G000059624

The Company of Laid Down Lovers

Jane Gibbs

Scripture quotations marked (TPT) are from The Passion Translation®. Copyright © 2017, 2018 by Passion & Fire Ministries, Inc. Used by permission. All rights reserved. ThePassionTranslation.com.

Scripture quotations marked (NIV) are taken from the Holy Bible, New International Version®, NIV®. Copyright © 1973, 1978, 1984, 2011 by Biblica, Inc.™ Used by permission of Zondervan. All rights reserved worldwide. www.zondervan.com The "NIV" and "New International Version" are trademarks registered in the United States Patent and Trademark Office by Biblica, Inc.™

Scripture quotations marked (AMP) are taken from the Amplified Bible, Copyright © 1954, 1958, 1962, 1964, 1965, 1987 by The Lockman Foundation. Used by permission.

Scripture quotations marked (ESV) are from The ESV® Bible (The Holy Bible, English Standard Version®), copyright © 2001 by Crossway, a publishing ministry of Good News Publishers. Used by permission. All rights reserved.

ISBN-13: 9798713282219

Editing & cover design: Mary King
Cover artwork: Jane Gibbs
Publisher: Jane Gibbs

Contents

Acknowledgements

My thanks go to Mary King for all your help in getting this book published. Your expertise, patience and hard work is greatly valued.

I also want to thank my husband Stuart, for his constant love and care over the years as we walked this life's journey together, and also to my beloved friends with whom I have walked life's path with. Thank you for loving me on my worst days and believing the best in me. You truly have loved me despite my brokenness and loved me in the midst of my storms.

With a special thanks to Jackie King and Liz Langley, who helped me to understand my true identity and become the woman of God I am today. You are such treasures sent from Heaven.

Mostly I want to give thanks to my beautiful Saviour and King, my constant Companion and Friend. You are the true hero of this book and of my life.

I dedicate this Book to You, King Yeshua.

Introduction

This book is about my journey and I hope your journey too. It's an opportunity for the soul to join the spirit man and abide in Him. It starts with lying down on the altar of sacrifice. This is not a swift death but a lifelong operation, where the Perfect Surgeon cuts away every part of us that doesn't belong in the hearts of those created in His image.

This is an invitation to journey with Him and reach His heart with ours. It begins with a call and a wooing; it becomes a connection. It's a journey of intimacy and the destination is friendship with God. This is our destiny, our purpose, our identity.

"God will continually revitalize you, implanting within you the passion to do what pleases him." Philippians 2:13 (TPT)

There isn't a set of instructions or a to-do list here, for that would be law. No, this is about a relationship with the living God where we choose to surrender. He gives us everything we need and empowers us to live a surrendered life for Him. He even provides us with the desire to pursue and be pursued!

You'll find recurring themes within these pages. Sometimes we need to hear the truth more than once so it settles within our hearts and transforms our minds. My hope is that you'll be encouraged and provoked to leave behind the old ways of self and find the relationship you were created to have. My life is a story of reaching God and learning how to walk and work with Him, being fully restored back to the Father, Son and Holy Spirit.

"To truly know him meant letting go of everything from my past... so that I may be enriched in the reality of knowing Jesus Christ and embrace him as Lord in all his greatness." Philippians 3:8 (TPT)

In this verse, we are urged to forget the past which has taught us so many valuable lessons. It's full of beautiful memories and painful wounds, but doesn't define us or our present. We shouldn't dwell on the failures, successes, or even the traumas of the past. We are to run straight for the Divine invitation of reaching the Heavenly goal and gaining the victory-prize through the anointing of Jesus.

As we run toward this goal and allow His embrace, it's He that heals our wounds and soothes our hurting souls. We no longer need to walk in coping strategies, wearing masks or following religious rules. The Holy Spirit reveals these masks and strategies. He heals us and teaches us to walk without them, leaning on Him every step of the way.

"I haven't yet acquired the absolute fullness that I'm pursuing, but I run with passion into his abundance so that I may reach the purpose that Jesus Christ has called me to fulfill and wants me to discover...
I forget all of the past... I run straight for the divine invitation of reaching the heavenly goal and gaining the victory-prize through the anointing of Jesus." Philippians 3:12-14 (TPT)

The prize is Him in all His glory and fullness. It is His smile as He looks intently into my eyes.

It is His wrap-around Presence as He embraces and surrounds me.

It is His delight and pleasure bursting the banks of my little soul.

It is Him overwhelming and overtaking my heart.

My Story

I want to share my story to give you the context of my journey, in the hope it may resonate with you and create a hunger to join me on the journey into the heart of God. I was created as a passionate, intense and fiery woman with a great capacity for love, but my unmet needs were too much for my young and inexperienced parents.

The events of my childhood created wounds only God could heal. In my teens, I embraced unforgiveness and bitterness for a time. My soul felt rotten and I despised it. Then, Jesus entered my life with His overwhelming, unconditional love. It floored me and I surrendered.

He and I have fought many times over the years. He's wrestled me from all the lies I believed about who I am and who He is. He knocked on the closed doors in me with persistence and always in love. He wasn't put off by the ugliness I despised. And so began His wooing of my heart.

As I look back on my life, I can see that God was relentlessly pursuing me from the beginning. He wants all of me and it's evident as He continues His pursuit. He is the perfect parent, correcting, guiding and nurturing me.

Your story may sound different with other challenges faced, but the truth is we all have locked doors we refuse to open due to pain, shame, disappointment or regret, yet God relentlessly pursues each and every one of us. We get to accept the Lover of our souls and hear His voice calling us deeper and higher. We can embrace the song sung over our lives or we can ignore it.

At the start of my Christian walk, I tried so hard to be obedient because I wanted to please God. I hadn't grasped that His unconditional love wasn't like the human love I'd known, including the conditional love I had for myself. At that time, I didn't understand His heart was always turned toward me, regardless of me! I heard words such as 'obedience', 'sacrifice' and 'surrender' from such a place of fear that I would dread listening or reading about these subjects, yet my heart yearned to please God. The journey from fear to love began.

My surrender came in my weakness and inability to reach God on my own. As I allowed God into my brokenness, I became strong. My true identity began to emerge and I understood that I affected God's heart deeply with my love for Him. I still yearn to please His heart, but it's from a place of knowing I am His beloved. I now choose surrender as an act of love and not from a place of fear.

The hardest and biggest hurdles I faced throughout the years were my own thoughts and feelings about myself. Self-forgiveness was a path I needed to take to be restored. I'd picked up so many lies about who I was that they shouted over any truth I was trying to grasp. I'd taken on board things shouted at me and spoken over me, as well as the treacherous whispers echoed within. I accepted them as the truth and I despised who I was.

Some of the core lies I believed were: *If I'm rejected by others is that not because I'm unworthy? If I'm ignored, overlooked or badly treated, is that not because I'm bad, ugly or disgusting? If I get what I deserve and am badly treated, isn't that because I deserve it?*

Self-rejection made it impossible for the love and affection showered upon me to reach my core, which needed so desperately to be loved. Even when I was reading and hearing about unconditional love, it didn't register within the chambers of my heart because I still loved myself conditionally. I operated in perfectionism, hated failure and would mentally torture myself over and over again.

If someone found out about any of my faults or criticised me, I would spiral into an emotional wreck. In all of this, God's love flowed towards me. The Father spoke softly into my heart, reminding me of the things He loved about me.

He sent people with words of love and encouragement, and friends who saw the best in me. As I allowed Him to unpick the web of lies that had grown up around my heart, the flickers of hope and joy that He placed inside of me from the very beginning set a flame alight inside.

Sleeping Beauty slept under a spell while thorny bushes grew up around her, making the path to her impenetrable. Imprisoned and hidden from the outside world, none but the bravest could attempt to reach her. Only the prince made his way to her side, awakening her with a kiss. This was true for me; it's true for all of us.

Only King Jesus was able to make His way past the thorns in my heart and awaken me with His kiss of revelation.[1] This gentle revelation awakens love within us. This is the King who fights for our hearts, bringing us to our knees in gratitude and love. I'm very grateful He opened my heart so that His torrents of love overwhelmed me and I could allow the flower of forgiveness to flourish.

I believe it's vital to operate in self-forgiveness so we can be transformed into the beings we were truly created to be, and not allow the enemy to devour us any longer. I traded all my shame for His holiness and righteousness and now stand within the walls of His truth. I stand within Him. My life now is to look at myself and see what He sees, to look in the mirror and see Him reflecting back. It's to accept what He says and reject anything that doesn't sound like His truth spoken over my life.

I must silence every voice that sounds like accusation and condemnation. This is the battle we all face to overcome our minds.

We are to be transformed by the renewing of our minds, not just to avoid sinful choices but believe the truth of who we really are! We need to replace every lie that is killing us and robbing our identity, with the truth.

"So now the case is closed. There remains no accusing voice of condemnation against those who are joined in life-union with Jesus, the Anointed One. For the "law" of the Spirit of life flowing through the anointing of Jesus has liberated us from the "law" of sin and death. For God achieved what the law was unable to accomplish, because the law was limited by the weakness of human nature. Yet God sent us his Son in human form to identify with human weakness. Clothed with humanity,

God's Son gave his body to be the sin-offering so that God could once and for all condemn the guilt and power of sin. So now every righteous requirement of the law can be fulfilled through the Anointed One living his life in us. And we are free to live, not according to our flesh, but by the dynamic power of the Holy Spirit!" Romans 8:1-4 (TPT)

We can therefore live a higher life, with a renewed mind from a place of truth in our real identity. God has done everything to put an end to the noisy rattle of the enemy's lies and accusations. All condemnation, whether it be from ourselves or others, is silenced.

Condemnation comes from Satan, who feasts on our fears and hides waiting to operate in the unredeemed parts of us. He sits in the darkness, thinking he's unnoticed until the light of revelation exposes him and his schemes. The Holy Spirit calls him out and at his exposure, we say, "The case is closed! I am not condemned!".

The enemy is silenced and we hear the voice of God as He tenderly speaks over us, explaining again our identity. We meet who we really are and accept the true us. We are washed clean and filled with light. It's from this place we're called to live, not from fleshly striving or good intentions but empowered by the Spirit of God as a son, led by Him to glory.

All we're asked to do is submit and surrender. This is glorious salvation! This is my story. It's the story of every human heart that travels from fear to love, reaching the reality that we are all beloved. Can you hear God knocking on the closed doors of your own heart?

The truth is, once our hearts have been ravished, overwhelmed and wooed, the step of laying it all down before Him in adoration comes from a pure heart of love. We know our needs are met regardless; our surrender is a response. It's the closest we get to offering unconditional love to Him.

My Life For You

My spirit and my heart say "Yes"

For in You I have all things.

In You I walk in peace and light,

Even in the darkness

Nothing is hidden from Your sight.

If I open up my hidden parts,

Those places secret, in the dark,

Your purity and goodness

Can come and abide within.

Your beauty marinating the dusty, dry spaces,

Drenching my soul in unapproachable light

That pure thoughts and holy desires,

May take the place of sin.

So, I open wide the door of my heart

To the glory of my King

Unhindered by the dead man

Alive to God and dead to him.

I choose to dwell in the Presence

For the world snaps at my heels,

It would trip me up if I gave it a chance.

Yet You woo me into the secret place and say,

"Come and abide, let's dance".

So, I open my heart to hear Your voice

To live for the audience of One.

No performance for the crowd

But romanced by the Son.

---

[1] "This Spirit kiss is what made Adam, the man of clay, into a living expression of God. Dust and deity met when the Maker kissed His Spirit wind into Adam. The Word of God is the kiss from the mouth of our Beloved, breathing upon us the revelation of His love." Simmons, B. (2017). *The Passion Translation New Testament with Psalms, Proverbs, and Song of Songs*. Minneapolis: Broadstreet Publishing Group, Song of Songs 2:1, p.291.

Divine Destiny

"Now, if anyone is enfolded into Christ, he has become an entirely new creation. All that is related to the old order has vanished. Behold, everything is fresh and new." 2 Corinthians 5:17 (TPT)

When we look at this verse, we need to understand what is old and what is being made new. We don't lose ourselves, no! It's all false identity that we leave behind. We don't deny who we are but disentangle from and renounce all that we are not. It's as we allow ourselves to be enfolded into Christ that He then redeems, transforms and makes us new.

The enfolding sets us free from our old life of sin, bad choices, negative behaviour patterns, unhealed wounds, the power of Satan, religious works, trying to please God and all fear-based conformity. We also leave behind our previous relationship with the world and our old mindsets.

We are not just reformed or patched up with a new set of rules to live by. We are liberated to live in union with Christ, making room for the Holy Spirit to dwell within us as our constant Companion and Helper. It's as we live in union with Christ that the old self dies and we emerge clean and beautiful, looking like our Father and Creator, as the image-bearers that we are.

This is our Divine destiny, to be face-to-face with God and bearing His image to the world. As we live out our lives here on Earth, we reflect the glory of who He is and His nature and character shine from our lives.

If you struggle to comprehend what it looks like to be enfolded into Christ, imagine yourself snuggled into Him. Let Him embrace you on your good days and bad days. We can live snuggled into God, allowing Him to take good care of us. He is available every moment of every day.

"Now it's time to be made new by every revelation that's been given to you. And to be transformed as you embrace the glorious Christ-within as your new life and live in union with him!" Ephesians 4:23-24 (TPT)

So, what is it to be made new? It's simply that we are dead and the King now lives and reigns within us. We are to bow down and submit every part of us to His majesty and sovereign rule in our lives. When I look at my old life and say, "The old has gone and the new has come", I know with confidence that there's no shame attached to my past because it's been crucified.

We may have been manipulated and controlled by the enemy but no more, for we are dead and Christ rules and lives in us. Therefore, as a new creation, we're no longer who we once believed ourselves to be. We are reborn. This is true for every one of us who've chosen to surrender to Christ. The crumbling buildings that were our lives are dismantled brick by brick, lovingly restored and fashioned, to be rebuilt in the Architect's original design.

Parts of us will look the same while some are completely unrecognisable to what they once were. Other parts will be similar but washed, cleaned and restored. There is no bulldozer demolition, for we are too precious to God and our hearts are so very sacred to Him. Every area in us that doesn't know or understand this truth needs to be quieted with His love, as His rest and peace transform the aching places of our hearts.

He allows the bruises to heal and changes the dressing on our wounds until we are ready to stand restored. Most importantly is to allow the joy-spring that's been released inside of us to gush forth and pour out. Where there once was sorrow, there now shall be rivers of joy. We can let courage, faith and hope overtake us as we stand to our full stature and reflect Him. This means that everything He is, so we are.

We are being made new by every revelation He gives us. By definition, a revelation is a thing revealed. In this instance, it is a truth that God reveals to our hearts personally. We'll begin to know our real identity deep within ourselves, as much as we know our own name.

A revelation is an understanding like we've never had before. It reminds me of when I suddenly understood fractions; we can be told something over and over, and we can practise and practise, and then one day we just know and understand. Therefore, once we have this revelation, we can let it transform our lives from the inside out. We live in union with Him, Bride and Bridegroom: beloved, held and chosen. This is our new life.

What is this new identity? We are His glory-carriers, we are His children, we are peaceful, we are humble, we are beloved, we are fearless, we are free, we are clean, we are held, we are pure, we are heirs and co-heirs, we are chosen, we are sons, we are brides, we are victorious, we are royal, we are strong, we are safe, we are embraced, we are righteous, we are joyful, we are holy. We know this because everything that Christ Jesus is, so are we.

We are His reflection and bear His image. This means we look like Him the more we are transformed. When people see us, they see Jesus. When we see Jesus, we see our true selves reflecting back at us. This is our identity and anything that contradicts this truth is a lie and a mutation of who we really are! Therefore, let's go forward in our true identity, moving from glory to glory in ever-increasing measure.

We constantly grow more like Him the more we surrender. There are no religious rules or works of man that could earn us what we already own. Let's embrace the free gift offered, our true nature and His Divine love. Receive today your restored identity that was won back for you at the Cross, and listen to the voice of the Father as He speaks over you who you really are.

Let His voice drown out the insulting, accusing and condemning lies that have been shouting within the walls of your heart from decades past. Renounce each one. If it doesn't come from the heart of the Father, then it simply isn't true. How do we know if it's the Father speaking over us? Simply this, if it sounds like love, lifts you up, gives you breath and causes you to feel at peace, then it is the Father.

Anything that brings you low and takes away from who you are is not Him. Even His correction brings love, self-acceptance and the ability to forgive. Hold up everything you hear and see to the light, for the light will reveal the truth. No darkness will stand where there is light. Let the Holy Spirit search every cavern of your heart to expose any pathway of pain so that you can be free to be you.

"You will be a crown of splendor in the Lord's hand, a royal diadem in the hand of your God. No longer will they call you Deserted, or name your land Desolate. But you will be called Hephzibah, and your land Beulah[2]; for the LORD will take delight in you." Isaiah 62:3-4 (NIV)

---

[2] Beulah' means to be married which is a covenant relationship; protected, provided for, no longer carrying the shame of widowhood, no longer abandoned. We have been given a name, are in an intimate relationship with Him, in mutual, joyful companionship.

Now We Are Mature

"When I was a child, I spoke about childish matters, for I saw things like a child and reasoned like a child. But the day came when I matured, and I set aside my childish ways." 1 Corinthians 13:11 (TPT)

What does it look like to set aside our childish ways? I don't believe the absence of childlike silliness or playfulness is the maturity being spoken of here, nor is it just the absence of childish tantrums or self-serving behaviours. A mature child of God is on a lifetime journey from orphan to sonship, death to life, darkness to light. We are to leave our childish ways and run to the throne room in our true identity.

One step of growth toward maturity is the choice to abide in the now and to live gratefully waiting for what is to come. It's important for all of us to posture our hearts in gratitude before God. I find that resting in God's Presence, allowing the Holy Spirit to direct me and meditating on all that is good and glorious, fills me with thankfulness.

But there have also been seasons of grudging resentment, where unfulfilled promises, unmet needs or other's behaviours, attitudes, opinions and thoughtless comments have invaded my thoughts and stolen my peace. If I stay there, then I stray from the pathway of gratitude and thankfulness.

I love God and have so much to be thankful for and I want to give Him all that I am, however, it's often the case that what I think and what He purposes don't always look the same. I'm human, and the unredeemed parts of me can gnaw away at my belief that God is good and that He always will be.

On one such occasion, God reminded me of the many times of ingratitude, frustration and resentment in my heart. He pointed out the many gifts I'd received, services that had been provided and love shown, that weren't what I wanted or hoped for. Basically, I was ungrateful and it stank. Ouch!

The Holy Spirit spoke gently to me and showed me in those moments how unloving it was and how hurtful I could be, after all, these were His beloved children. I need the Holy Spirit's help in those moments to be grateful and choose thankfulness. It's not just in the big tests of life, in struggles or suffering, but more often in the everyday moments.

In the big challenges, we easily throw ourselves on God's mercy. We run into Him, grateful for His protection and care, but it's often harder in the little things. I speak here of the niggles, irritations and frustrations we find in the everyday. It should be easy to be grateful towards such a gracious Father who has bestowed so much on all His creation, and sometimes it is.

In the times when grace flows from the throne and we see the bigger picture, we rise above the smallness of our own lives. At other times, it's a hard decision to let go of ourselves and choose gratitude despite unmet needs, undelivered promises and when we're let down or overlooked.

We have Him and all creation, which is given to us for our care. We have every blessing and the favour of Almighty God to enjoy, yet we so often forget this. It's in the moments of tiredness, busyness, pressure or stress that the test of gratitude becomes reality. Sometimes the prophecy and the promise are just too unviable, and God's answer seems so slow to deliver what He said He would.

In a time of next-day delivery, waiting for God seems interminable and very often the answer doesn't look like the picture we've built up in our minds. The lesson to wait patiently for the Lord has been hard-won in my life, yet so much growth comes in the waiting and walking in thankfulness.

In short, we have to counter the passionate desire for more of God and the expectation of all that He holds for us, with the gentle quietness of patiently waiting with childlike faith. The answer to our human state is simple; David says, *"I will yet praise him"* (Psalm 42:5 NIV) and *"I waited patiently for the Lord"* (Psalm 40:1 NIV).

I'm reminded of when we were planning a trip to New Zealand as a family. My husband spent many months planning our trip in detail: the excursions, where to visit, places to stay, etc. He painstakingly researched the best places that would suit the needs of all members of our family. He even organised the visas, spending money and passports; every detail was considered.

We seemed to be talking about it for a very long time, even with the date a long way off! He planned ahead for his family and as a good father, anticipated the needs of his children. My husband could have said, "I know the plans I have for you. They are good plans, you will love them". Does that sound familiar? This is the heart of our Heavenly Father planning ahead for us, ensuring everything is right and the timing perfect.

He says, *"I know the plans I have for you"* (Jeremiah 29:11 NIV). When the waiting goes on for years or even decades, we can grumble or we can sing out our gratitude. God is still faithful. Lifting our gaze to His throne is all we need to restore our thankfulness.

One of the biggest challenges when moving toward maturity is laying down our lives for Him. For many of us, we sing about total surrender and promise it over and over, but how often does the sacrifice keep getting off the altar? To go deep into God's heart is simple; it's a choice we get to make. It isn't always an easy one but a step by step, moment by moment pathway to Him, one that He walks with us. Jesus meets us and offers His hand to lead us to the Father's heart.

The boulders we hit along the way highlight our monuments of pain. Some of these monuments are idols or altars we sacrificed our peace on. They are familiar and have been with us for so long that we've accepted them as part of our identity.

We can fight God, wrestling to hold onto something that's toxic to our souls and is actually killing us, but in Christ we are victors over our past and our mistakes. They are there to teach us and cause growth but should not define who we are. Even the past successes we celebrate, proudly wearing our badges of ministry, status or human endeavour, can hinder us from understanding our true identity.

James Richards wrote a book called, 'How to Stop the Pain'[3], in which he explains it's our reaction to a situation, the judgments we make about that situation, and the response of others that can cause us pain. Taking offence, holding a grudge and unforgiveness, rub away at our hearts like salt in a wound. They are toxic to us mentally and emotionally and cause a breakdown in our relationship with others, ourselves and God.

It was a tough book to read but brought me understanding and healing. I learnt I wasn't subject to external forces but to my internal decisions. It wasn't an easy journey but the Holy Spirit walked with me step by step, with the gift of grace to choose forgiveness and gratitude, and also grace for those around me.

Unforgiveness became a price too high to pay because it cost me dearly. If we want heart-connection with God and reconciliation with ourselves, we need to live by the Kingdom principles of love. To live the old way is to live in the kingdom of the enemy, where we have to disengage and turn away from the Father. However, we can face up to what lurks in our own darkness.

Sometimes I'm shocked by what's revealed to me there but my gracious Father is never surprised, offended or put off, *"For nothing in all creation is hidden from God's sight"* (Hebrews 4:13 NIV). If we lay our lives down on the altar of self-sacrifice, then anything that stands up and refuses to surrender is already dead to us and impedes the flow of our spirit and His.

'Dying to self' is not punishment or denial of who we are, but a laying down of our old self. We are never asked to deny who we are; God exposes the lies of who we are not. All of us have believed words told to us by the father of lies, who wants to defraud us of our true identity.

The bad habits we need to lay down are often linked to a much stronger root. Somewhere inside of us is someone in need, who may be turning to social media for affirmation or food for nurture. In all of this, we still get to make moment by moment choices. The King will not excuse us for He is passionate about the redemption of our souls. Once we allow Him to reveal and heal the reason behind all our negative habits, reactions and failings, dying to self will be less of a battle.

We are not asked to self-flagellate, for Jesus took our beating and our death. We are asked to walk above our pain, unmet needs and current circumstances and say, "No", to the voice of self-gratification. We aren't asked to deny our pain or past but we also shouldn't wallow there; we just need to deal with those ghosts.

How many of us hide the shame of our darker moments? We wince when these are revealed to us, yet the Father of love looks straight into our eyes and sees only the sacrifice of His Son in that moment. His forgiveness is total and complete. It is we who struggle with forgiveness and unconditional love. Likewise, when we've been on the receiving end of someone else's mistakes or brokenness and the wounding is real, it can seem impossible to forgive and release the other person from the debt owed to us.

The Father understands our pain. He is not excusing any injustice but looks at that person with love and sees the Cross. Can we come to this place? Not denying our past or the injury from ourselves and others, but walking out forgiveness in truth. This is true love.

When I met Jesus, I knew He had forgiven me. I understood that He loved me and went to the Cross for me, but I just couldn't love myself. The stench of shame, fear, regret and the belief that I was 'bad' was too much for me. He loved, nurtured and cared for me deeply, forgiving everything, but I couldn't quite let go.

I stank, yet Jesus never flinched! The Holy Spirit spent years unravelling the knots to separate the lies and unbelief from the truth, searching for the treasure He knew had been placed inside of me by the Father. It was He who began to reveal the gold within. The truth is that the Father has placed treasure inside every human heart, that includes you and me. There is gold inside every one of us.

I know this because the Word says we are made in His image for His good pleasure! The Holy Spirit is waiting to disentangle our real selves from the mutated creatures we allowed ourselves to become. That is true salvation. He wants to show us where we fit in the story of eternity. When we open our hearts fully in this way, He can dwell in the space that was vacated by the evicted, old, false self. He desires to live there.

For me, my restored past doesn't change the facts of what happened, but it heals the wounds and becomes my story. My scarred heart and His scarred body tell the story of redemption to the world. This is my testimony and it's Good News.

I remember expressing my love for God during a time of intimacy and devotion one day, and asking Him to dwell within me and reign in my life, and I meant it! However, it wasn't long before a situation I was facing began to overwhelm me. It loomed up in front of me and the hopeless voice grew louder and louder. I felt alone, weary and helpless.

I crawled onto the sofa, my heart reaching for His. After soaking with the Holy Spirit, my peace and equilibrium returned but as I sat before the Lord I felt a sense of failure, rebuking myself for my inconsistent heart. What He said surprised me. He knew what would happen and had allowed it! He engineered that moment for He knew it was already hidden away within me. It was a voice that needed to be heard and healed.

He wanted to dwell within my heart but He would not share the space with my attitude or pain. He wanted it out of the house for both our sakes, a bit like taking out the bins. It's not sin I'm talking of here, but anything that doesn't match up with the identity and character He created. He now does this often with me.

We can be there at the altar, willing and trying to die to self and live for Him the best we can, but our fears and selfish ambitions pervade the air with their toxic fumes. We can't hide them and sooner or later we have to sort them out. Doing this is simply to nail them to the Cross, for they don't belong in the hearts of God's children.

"My old identity has been co-crucified with Messiah and no longer lives; for the nails of his cross crucified me with him. And now the essence of this new life is no longer mine, for the Anointed One lives his life through me—we live in union as one! My new life is empowered by the faith of the Son of God who loves me so much that he gave himself for me, and dispenses his life into mine!" Galatians 2:20 (TPT)

The Father never asks us to 'try to die', He simply asks us to surrender, to choose what He would choose and to love with His love. If we want to love Him with all our heart, mind, soul and strength, the fragmented, dark spaces that are in rebellion, unbelief or fear, and the parts that hold onto apathy or hatred come as well; that is what gets sacrificed on the altar.

Choosing to love and surrender, even in our pain and brokenness, is such sweetness to Him. Letting go of any debt and receiving the perfect love of a passionate King who stood in the gap for every wrong word or action, is what He asks of His beloved. We know self-promotion and pride have to die, but so do self-protection and self-deprecation. Those things died with Christ and we receive unconditional love from Him to love ourselves and others. We are to fix our gaze on the Author and Perfecter of our faith and simply adore Him.

Another step toward maturity is understanding true beauty: His and ours. *"Let your true beauty come from your inner personality, not a focus on the external."* (1 Peter 3:3-4 TPT). As we focus on and take time in the internal life with Him, our true beauty will shine for He is our true beauty.

In today's society, a lot of importance has been attributed to outward beauty. The celebrity culture has driven an idolisation of outward perfection with endless diets and expensive, cosmetic surgeries. I don't want to explore the destructive effect this has had but rather, I want to highlight this false idea of beauty and look to what God considers beautiful. Of course, some people have been blessed with outward beauty but this is a gift and is not meant to be worshipped or envied.

"Man looks to the outer appearance but God looks to the heart" 1 Samuel 16:7 (ESV)

The Godhead pays little attention to our outward appearance for He is looking intently into our hearts. We have been lied to by the enemy, believing our self-worth and acceptance of each other hinges on the pursuit of this lie. The ever-changing face of worldly beauty is a cruel master who is impossible to please and doesn't value what's beneath.

The thief comes to steal our identity and has created this false idol. He lies to us, shouting from the media platforms, hoping to drown out the truth that every human being created is beautiful. Regardless of the shape of our face, body size, height or gender, we are fearfully and wonderfully made. As an example, if you think, *I hate the shape of my nose,* then take a look at this fact about this wonderful creation:

"Air comes into the body through the nose. As it passes over the specialized cells of the olfactory system, the brain recognizes and identifies smells. Hairs in the nose clean the air of foreign particles. As air moves through the nasal passages, it is warmed and humidified before it goes into the lungs."[4]

How fearfully and wonderfully made! Or maybe you hate your thighs? If you can walk, run, jump, bend, climb, stand or dance, then you can thank your thighs for their strength and support. Our bodies are a creative marvel and God put a lot of thought into designing us.

Let's look at what God's Word says about our beauty; *"He adorns the humble with His beauty"* (Psalm 149:4 TPT). When we walk in humility, He adorns us with His beauty. This means we can't produce beauty on our own merit. What the Lord calls 'beauty' cannot be manufactured by us; our good deeds are as filthy rags.

We come to Him in a humble posture, admitting that without Him even our best efforts need to be cleansed with His holiness and righteousness. He sees our filthy rags and even our nakedness and adorns us with Himself. The Father looks at us through Christ and sees His beauty reflected back. He calls us beautiful.

The King says to the Bride in Song of Songs 4:7 (TPT), *"Every part of you is so beautiful, my darling. Perfect is your beauty, without flaw within"*. He says that to every single one of us. He calls our beauty perfect, without flaw! We are made in His image and carry His attributes within us. When God created man, He saw that it was good.

When He created you and me, when He fashioned us in the womb, when He chose our abilities, gifts, characteristics and uniqueness, He said, "It is good". When He chose your personality and your body shape, He said, "It is good". If He is beauty and we are made in His image, then we are beauty too. However, this beauty gets disfigured by the ravages of sin, shame, lies and deceit.

The defilement of our souls builds up layers upon layers of resentment, unforgiveness, fear and control, which all hide the real us. When we are hidden under all this ugliness, we believe the lies because they look true. Jesus washes away all sin, shame and iniquity, to reveal a pure, righteous heart before God, yet He waits for our permission to do this.

As we look into the eyes of our Father and we allow love to begin chipping away at the crust of our hearts, it's possible to believe the truth. These clay jars house our inner beauty as co-heirs, kings, sons, lovers and image-bearers of our Creator.

We only need to give the Holy Spirit permission to go mining into our depths and pull out the treasures He's placed within us. Then, when He reveals to us who we are, we can declare our true identity before the throne of God in gratitude and confidence. As we allow this process and our eyes are finally opened, we can see God in us and can begin to see God in each other. I praise God for the people in my life who've seen Him in me and called it forth. I can now stand and declare that I am beautiful.

Our beauty comes not from our outward appearance but that we house the Glory of God within. The Holy Spirit meets our spirit man here within our flesh, so who are we to condemn it? The Word of God speaks of beauty as submission, surrender, worship, adoration, devotion, passion and love.

Our beauty comes from our submission and decision to choose Him above all else, to worship His splendour, to adore Him and adorn ourselves with His attributes as we humble ourselves before Him. We were all created to worship, it's integral to being human. But it's *what* we choose to worship that counts. I believe this is the beauty God looks for, the beauty that Christ looks for in His Bride.

We become His beauty as we allow Him to reign and shine within us. We carry His attributes of mercy, kindness, gentleness, courage and holiness. He calls His beauty ours. He looks deep within us to our heart of hearts and when He finds our worship, adoration and awe of Him, He rejoices and shouts, "It is good!". The world's pursuit of outward beauty and even of good works, will not lead us to the beauty fit for a Bride at the altar with the Bridegroom.

If we lay our hearts down before His Divine beauty and surrender the pursuit of anything that doesn't lead to Him, then we will be *"transformed by the glorious Christ within"* (Ephesians 4:24 TPT). Simply put, we know our physical form by looking at our reflection in a mirror, however, we see our identity as we look at Jesus, who reflects who we truly are.

God's Word reveals His description of us as His beloved ones who are wonderfully and fearfully made, and as we sit with the Holy Spirit, He gives us understanding and revelation of God's beauty and ours.

Let's consider the beauty of Christ; a man so badly beaten He was unrecognisable, just one lash away from death, His skin horribly torn. His body was stripped, bloody and cursed. Dying a shameful death that wasn't His own, before jeering crowds He released forgiveness to mankind with His last, few breaths.

What a beautiful Man; what a beautiful Saviour. He made Himself ugly, taking our defilement, sin, rebellion and hatred so that our beauty could be restored. He took our ugliness into Hell so that we could step into Heaven with His beauty and sit with Him. His mercy, compassion, holiness and sacrifice are so incredibly, breathtakingly beautiful.

---

[3] Richards, J. (2001). *How to Stop the Pain*. New Kensington: Whitaker House.
[4] Healthline Editorial Team. (2018). *Nose*. New York: Healthline Medical Network.

Relationship

God desires relationship with us above all things. He pursues our hearts as the perfect Father; He makes the way and constantly calls us gently to Himself. He waits patiently to open our eyes to see what's been right in front of us from the beginning. The Father wants restoration with His children. The Creator wants connection with His creation. The Bridegroom wants union with His Bride and He calls out, "Where are you?".

"And they heard the sound of the LORD God walking in the garden in the cool of the day, and the man and his wife hid themselves from the presence of the LORD God among the trees of the garden. But the LORD God called to the man and said to him, 'Where are you?'" Genesis 3:8-9 (ESV)

God created man, the pinnacle of His creation, made in His image to be His children. Mankind was not spoken into being like the rest of creation. God could have just called us forth but no, He caressed the earth, lovingly weaving and knitting our intricate bodies into being. Then He breathed His life into us. He kissed us alive, poured in His character and image and called us 'man'.

This is the beginning of the love-relationship, right at the start of the Bible. In Genesis 3, we see the breaking of this relationship and God calling out, "Where are you?". Adam and Eve were hiding in shame and the Father was heartbroken. "Where are you my son, my heart, my joy?".

He wasn't looking for a 'factual' answer for He knew where they were. The Father calls the same question throughout eternity to every human heart. Every time we hide, look away or find satisfaction and gratification in something other than Him, His heart

41

calls out to ours. Every time we choose independence or control, when we don't look for Him and His heart, He calls out to us.

He always knows where we are. He knows all our hiding places and knows better than we do why we go there. His ultimate desire is a relationship and He makes it possible in every way to rescue and maintain that relationship. He chose to become part of us as a man and died our death. He did everything necessary so that when He calls out to us, we can come running in the way made accessible by Him.

Even in our sin-drenched state, our inadequacies and rebellion, with nothing to qualify us for His Presence, we can come. Our qualification is that we are His sons and He delights in us. He never forces us to love Him or bow the knee before Him. He is a loving Father longing for His children, a Bridegroom calling out to His Bride, "Where are you?".

There may be places in our hearts where we feel lost to God, hiding from Him. The Father stands waiting every day, looking for the weary and prodigal areas of our hearts to appear over the horizon so that He can lavish on us the cloak of His covering and the ring of sonship that's been rightfully restored to us at such great cost. He calls for a feast as joy explodes within His heart and we are lost in the embrace of His perfect, Fathering love.

I never knew my biological father and spent many of my younger years with gaps in my identity, wondering about my heritage and where I fit. This is true for many people who haven't known one or both of their parents. We need to recognise who we are by understanding where we came from. My journey of finding myself wasn't by finding my earthly father, but finding my Heavenly Father. He knew me, He disciplined me and taught me about myself.

He showed me my heritage and led me from orphan to son. It's the same for all of us. Whether we have met our parents or not and whatever our relationship with them is, we all need to be restored back to our Heavenly Father to understand who we are. We need to be parented by Him to leave our orphan state and be embraced as beloved sons.

When we first surrender to God at the point of our salvation, we give ourselves to Him. However, it's a lifetime process of surrendering and answering His cry with, "Here I am!". His love, compassion and desire for us woo us in and surrender becomes easy. He justifies and edifies us, and we surrender and love Him while we are embraced in His unconditional love.

For some of us, we aren't so much lost to God but have lost ourselves. It's as we come to Him that He finds *us* and we are restored to our true selves. This is what it means to begin understanding your identity as His beloved child. As we are found by Him, we find ourselves in His heart. As we look to who He is and spend time in His Presence, listening and letting Him love us, we find who we are.

It's from this restored state that we can stand on Mount Zion and love Him with our whole selves, worshipping in spirit and in truth. Let's not wait. This is a continual process; as we love and worship Him, we are restored, and as we are restored, we again choose to love and worship Him. This cycle goes on and on as more of our hearts are found and redeemed.

The God of all Heaven and Earth is calling you today, "Where are you, my beloved child?". Can you hear Him? Once we respond to the call, we begin the journey to His heart. What is our response to this love-cry?

"O God of my life, I'm lovesick for you in this weary wilderness. I thirst with the deepest longings to love you more, with cravings in my heart that can't be described. Such yearning grips my soul for you, my God! I'm energized every time I enter your heavenly

sanctuary to seek more of your power and drink in more of your glory. For your tender mercies mean more to me than life itself.

How I love and praise you, God! Daily I will worship you passionately and with all my heart. My arms will wave to you like banners of praise. I overflow with praise when I come before you, for the anointing of your presence satisfies me like nothing else. You are such a rich banquet of pleasure to my soul. I lie awake each night thinking of you and reflecting on how you help me like a father.

I sing through the night under your splendor-shadow, offering up to you my songs of delight and joy! With passion I pursue and cling to you. Because I feel your grip on my life, I keep my soul close to your heart... These liars will be silenced forever! But with the anointing of a king I will dance and rejoice along with all his lovers who trust in him." Psalm 63:1-8,11 (TPT)

My response to this passage is that as I worship and love God with all my heart and life, and as I choose humility and allow my heart to become teachable and pliable, so I will be energised, empowered, anointed and fully satisfied. I will see and experience His glory. This needs to be our motivation, the steering of our hearts and lives, our only agenda. The Holy Spirit helps us for He knows us intimately.

We can smile at this truth for we know we have a constant Companion, Friend and Mentor. We should no longer be consumed or entertained by the smallness of our minds, the petty slights, the worries of today, the grumbles within, not even the humdrum of everyday life. No, we can walk the higher pathway, the company of the Holy Spirit day by day, moment by moment, and to continually lift our gaze on God Most High.

We are to persistently make our thoughts lofty. Our purpose, bigger than any dream or plan that God has for us, is to thirst with the deepest longings of love for Him. Our purpose is not to crave the things of this world but His Presence, and for this yearning to grip our souls.

There we will be energised. There we will seek more of Him, not because we wish to be powerful but to embrace His heart and sit in close relationship with Him. Then we will understand who we are and who we are not.

Do we overflow with praise in every situation like David? Do we long for God's Presence and call Him a "rich banquet of pleasure" to our souls? Are we awake at night, thinking of Him and reflecting on His Fathering? Do we offer songs of delight and joy? Can we say that we pursue and cling to God with passion? Do we keep our souls close to the heart of God?

It's as we allow God deeper into our heart of hearts that we will cry out like David did. This is not a list of how to pursue God but a heart cry that is lovesick with longing. You may say, "But my troubles are not petty and it's not fickleness of heart but great pressures and struggles that take my attention". God understands this and yet He calls us higher; He calls us home.

David was a man who made mistakes. He was a shepherd boy and an outcast who became a man on the run for his life. He was a murderer and an adulterer but David moved the heart of God because he pursued His heart. This is our destiny and purpose. It's where we belong and why we were created. We weren't called primarily to be bank managers, shop keepers, teachers, parents, prophets or pastors; our vocations and careers all come after loving the heart of God with our whole being.

Living from the Father's Lap

Several years ago, I had an encounter with the Father where I received healing in an area of pain from my childhood and He restored the place in my heart that had felt fatherless. In the encounter, I was allowed to climb upon the Father's lap as a little child, resisting fear and receiving love.

The Father listened as I freely and honestly spoke out my pain without fear of rebuke or punishment. He restored me in that moment. I felt safe and secure in a way I never had before. The Father never said I had to leave but I got off His lap to go and live my busy life.

A few years later, during a time of trial for my family, the Holy Spirit said to me, "It is time to live from the Father's lap". I began to dialogue with the Holy Spirit, working out what this would look like as a lifestyle. I knew the Father hadn't changed; His protection, promises and character would always be the same. His safety and intimacy are the same today as in that encounter.

When circumstances, seasons, other people or my own heart throw a curveball, I can rest back into Him. Even after such an encounter, I still need to be reminded to return and live from that place. The Father is constant, it is I that keep leaving and returning! The Father searches and waits with longing for the prodigal parts of our hearts, the parts that are far off, afraid, living in our mess, rebellious, broken and disconnected.

"So the young son set off for home. From a long distance away, his father saw him coming, dressed as a beggar, and great compassion swelled up in his heart for his son who was returning home. So the father raced out to meet him. He swept him up in his arms, hugged him dearly, and kissed him over and over with tender love." Luke 15:20 (TPT)

This passage is often used in the context of those who've known and loved God and then abandoned Him for whatever reason. We understand that the Father is waiting expectantly for their return, and He is. We miss the fact that we can all have far off, rebellious parts inside of us that refuse to submit and receive His love.

We can also decide that even when we return we must be a servant. We think that we'd never be considered a son because of our shame and yet the Father desires to fully restore us, if only we would let Him. He wants the unfathered places of our souls that are orphaned and hiding.

For many of us, even though we know the Father, there are parts inside of us that have never known His Fathering or unconditional love. He yearns for those places. He looks for the dark spaces in us and says, "I sent My Son to die for that moment, that memory, that situation. He died for the trauma you've felt, for the choices you've made and the choices others have made that caused wounding and brokenness". He allows you to leave through free will but He longs for your return.

More recently, God said to me, "I wait for you to quiet your heart, to turn your gaze toward me, to give Me your attention, for I have things to say, secrets to share and truths to reveal. I want to remind you of My promises, My character and My heart toward you. My gaze is on you and you have My attention. So, let's talk. Let's meet together and commune together. You are part of My plan for this world, so come and be part of the plan".

This is the heart of the Father towards His children. Our response should be to quiet our hearts and minds before Him, allowing Him to visit us and arrest our thoughts, emotions and plans. He wants us to know His thoughts and make them our thoughts so we are consumed by Him. It's easy to become distracted in a world full of noise. There is so much vying for our attention, we have to run for cover from the bombardment on our senses.

We can also easily slip into old mindsets and allow the dead man to chatter away. My response in those moments is, "Yes Lord. I want to sit on your knee, ready to learn from You, Papa". Even as I write I'm convicted in my soul, knowing that I don't always live in this place. How can the Father reveal His plans, purposes and secrets to us unless we come and sit with Him?

As a family, when we had to discuss anything with our children, we would bring it up as we sat around the dinner table. If we weren't able to do that, we would call them together to sit with us. To this day, we ensure the relationships between us and our children are working and we keep the communication channels open. How much more does the Father long to discuss His plans with us?

His wisdom and direction are always perfect, always truth and are always for our good. His intricate plans have us woven into them. You and I are part of the bigger picture! We need to have wisdom and understanding for ourselves in our own lives, but it goes further than that. As part of His family, we get to participate in the family business, partnering with King Jesus in bringing Heaven to Earth.

When the Father speaks, it is righteousness, holiness and wisdom, no brokenness, no human agenda, nothing that takes away from us but completes who we are. We are filled to overflowing. If we want to know His promises and plans for us and this world, then we need to sit on His knee ready to learn. By simply being immersed in the truth He speaks, our hearts and minds are protected from the lies of the enemy. No longer weary from the battles of life, we watch from the comfort of His lap as He fights for us.

"I am humbled and quieted in your presence. Like a contented child who rests on its mother's lap, I'm your resting child and my soul is content in you. O people of God, your time has come to quietly trust, waiting upon the Lord now and forever." Psalm 131:2-3 (TPT)

When I read this, I meditated on what it's like to be a small child, resting contentedly on their mother's lap. The child is safe and unconcerned, knowing her needs are met. She doesn't question if she should be there or if she's worthy. She doesn't ask herself if she is lovable or deserving. She isn't worried, fearful or restless. She feels her mother's warmth, smells her mother's familiar scent.

As she lays her head on her mother's chest, she can hear her heartbeat and feel the rise and fall of her breathing. She can also hear mother's voice resounding in her chest as she speaks. The sound literally vibrates through both of their bodies. This little child is out of reach from all her enemies and she cannot see or hear them.

We can choose to lie here! We can be humbled and quieted by God's love and Presence. We can be content, resting and quietly trusting. If we choose to live in this reality, our whole perception shifts and we are free to love as we are loved, free to give adoration back to Him. Those around us are blessed as they feel the warmth of the Father's love radiating off of us.

All that He asks will be a light burden; it will be a joy, a surrender in worship, a joyful sacrifice. He doesn't want painful obedience wrenched out of us under the rule of religion. I want to choose blissful surrender under the weight of overwhelming love, a child's choice to love freely. After all, this is the sacrifice the Lord desires.

It's as simple as fixing our gaze on Him and listening for His whisper. The word 'whisper' means to "speak using the breath but not the voice".[5] To hear a whisper, you need to be close and you need to lean in. Oh, to have the breath of God whispered into our hearts. We can walk through life attentive and sensitive, encountering Him. We can have His perspective on everything we see, hear and touch.

Our daily tasks will be thrilling for He will be there. When we rest back into love, into Him, then the bigger picture is exciting and not overwhelming. We can see the world through the eyes of the victors we are, which changes how we live and love. In all things, we have the opportunity to love from a place of rest in the Father, where loving ourselves and each other becomes much easier.

If we live in this place and love like this, we will find fulfilling the two greatest commandments given by Jesus easier as well; *"Love the Lord your God with every passion of your heart, with all the energy of your being, and with every thought that is within you… And the second is like it in importance: 'You must love your friend in the same way you love yourself"* (Matthew 22:37, 39 TPT).

The Father gives us everything we need to be part of this beautiful relationship with Him and with one another. Whatever He's given us to do should be from this place of the Father's love. The language of the Kingdom is love: Fatherly love, Bridal love and love laid down. Let us learn to become fluent in this language.

---

[5] *Cambridge International Dictionary of English.* (1995). Cambridge: Cambridge University Press.

Our Great Friend, the Holy Spirit

The Holy Spirit trains us in obedience by His guiding voice. He shows us the will of God, the longings of the Bridegroom and the heartbeat of our Father in Heaven. He writes His law on our hearts, which is our conscience and the moral code that runs through us. He speaks of God's judgement to correct us, keep us safe and help us walk in right relationship with Him, each other and ourselves.

He never condemns or punishes us but brings us into alignment with the mind of God. It's His discipline that trains us up as sons and co-heirs so that we can become trustworthy stewards of the Kingdom which He desires to share with us. The Holy Spirit comes to bring conviction, direction and wisdom. He reminds us of who we really are.

Like any good parent, He lets us know when we aren't being our best. As a mother, I've said to my children at times, "This behaviour or attitude is not who you are, you are better than this". It isn't from a place of embarrassment but a desire to guide my children to be the best they can be and abandon anything that isn't who they really are. This is true of the Holy Spirit. I would rather His conviction and correction than the miserable consequences of my bad choices!

The Holy Spirit is also the whisperer who encourages us to come away with our King. He gently nudges us to find a time and place to look up and to go deep. He sets ablaze the words of the Bible, causing our hearts to sing at the truths we find. He gives sight to our minds and wisdom to understand Almighty God. He fuels our creativity to bring forth songs, poems, art, sculptures, inventions and business ideas.

He truly is the best Companion we could have. In a world of uncertainty, it's good to know that He knows the way and has everything we need to get there. He empowers and infuses us with love, joy, peace, patience, kindness, goodness, faithfulness and gentleness (Galatians 5:22 ESV), for these are His fruits and He graciously and generously shares them with us. He never gives us fear, but *"mighty power, love, and self-control"* (2 Timothy 1:7 TPT).

We are His temple and He comes to dwell within us (1 Corinthians 6:19). He actively chooses to live inside our physical bodies and commune with our spirit. This is where the action is! This is where all our meetings take place. I cannot explain or hardly describe it, but I know this has been the journey of so many people who have befriended the beautiful Holy Spirit. It's from this relationship that we can live and move and have our being. We can do all that He asks of us as He leads us.

Jude 1:20 (TPT) says, *"constantly and progressively build yourselves up on the foundation of your most holy faith by praying every moment in the Spirit"*. If the Holy Spirit dwells inside every believer, He is available for continuous conversation and companionship as we walk through our lives. We can walk in tandem with Him in all things.

We can discuss every eventuality, every emotion and every thought process with the Lover of our souls. Every decision, situation, circumstance, setback or success is an opportunity to have a discussion with Him. It's in these times we ask advice or questions and express our emotions and thoughts to Him.

This leads me to the next verse which says, *"Fasten your hearts to the love of God"* (Jude 1:21 TPT). To fasten is to lock on and make secure. We aren't to let our emotions or thought processes untether us from God's love. We can be open and honest with the One who loves us best. In our greatest moments and our bleakest, plus every moment in between, we can live fastened and secured onto God's love.

Our emotions can deceive us but the truth about God's love remains. We can become misguided or believe lies through disappointment or pain, and yet we must call all our thoughts into alignment with the truth. The good news is that the Holy Spirit is our constant Companion and will always speak the truth in love, empowering us to remain fastened onto the Father and guiding us back to His heart if we stray.

The Seven Flames of Love

This chapter originates from a dream I had, where I saw a book called 'The Seven Flames of Love' and the Holy Spirit said He would give me these flames. When I awoke, I asked the Lord what it meant. I decided the first thing to do was read 1 Corinthians 13:4-8, which talks about the attributes of love. As I read and meditated on those verses, I wrote out what I believed the Lord was saying.

The Holy Spirit highlighted seven flames to me. There are of course other attributes and aspects to the character of God's love, but I believe this is what the Lord wanted me to share: patience, kindness, humility, honesty, honour, graciousness and generosity of spirit. I believe we all carry these attributes in differing measures.

Some people are more kind by nature, some more patient and so on, that is because we are all image-bearers of the Father and He has gifted us with different aspects of His character, whether we are redeemed or not! These gifts are to be celebrated in each other. The attributes we are blessed with do not negate us from becoming more like Him in our weaker areas.

We understand that as we allow the Holy Spirit to dwell within us, His fruits will be displayed because He empowers us for life and good works. There is no striving here, but our moment by moment choice to turn away from what we know is wrong, asking the Holy Spirit to blow through us and energise us to stand in the right decision with His strength and grace.

As with all God-attributes, they begin and end with Him. Whether it is our natural inclination or a choosing of His way over ours, it all comes from surrendering everything to Him and allowing Him to sit enthroned in our hearts, constantly inclining our ear to His voice and taking every opportunity to see what He sees.

As we dwell with the Holy Spirit, bringing all our choices, opinions and belief systems to Him, we will surprise ourselves as we see Him in our words and actions, especially in our responses to the people He has placed around us and any challenges faced.

Why 'flames' of love? The Lord desires that these attributes burn within us, that we'd give them fuel and not allow them to be quenched. When they are dying out or becoming embers, we are to fan them into flame. God helps us in this by breathing His life into us. We also help each other turn our flickers into flames; *"spur one another on toward love and good deeds"* (Hebrews 10:24 NIV).

This isn't a nagging preach but a championing cheer where we say to one another, "You are His image-bearer so allow the Spirit to love through you and burn brightly!". I am so grateful for those in my life who cheer me on and believe in the God in me. They encourage me to burn with His love.

In all this, I would encourage you that the Lord is not asking for perfection; He is asking for pursuit. He is asking us to love Him, each other and ourselves. He is asking us to fan the flames and burn, lighting the path to His heart that others may find the way. As we dwell more consistently in Him, we'll find that we naturally live from these attributes of love by allowing His nature to burn within us. Let's pursue this together so that all will see Him as He truly is.

Patience

"A waiting person is a patient person. The word patience means the willingness to stay where we are and live the situation out to the full in the belief that something hidden there will manifest itself to us." - Henri J.M. Nouwen[6]

To be patient is to let go of agendas, time scales and ideas of what the answer, breakthrough or healing will look like. Sitting alongside someone as they journey takes great patience because they may grow at a different rate or in a different way to us. If we're impatient with others, they won't learn any faster. In fact, the opposite can be true and they may falter in confidence.

We all need patience when learning to walk in new ways, break old habits and make good choices. We need to trust that God ultimately has it all in hand and has a plan and purpose for us. It may not look like it at first, but He does turn everything around for our good. When there seems to be no change or movement within ourselves or another, we need the Holy Spirit's wisdom to know when to push and when to rest, yield and trust.

I find this hardest within the context of family, whether as a daughter, a sister, a wife or a mother. There were times when my patience was sorely tested. Now I look back and see those tests have grown something inside of me that wouldn't be there otherwise. Family is a great place to learn about relationships and love. I'm sure there are many more opportunities to grow in patience and I'm grateful for the Holy Spirit's empowering Presence.

Kindness

What do you imagine when you think of someone who shows kindness? For me, one of the greatest kindnesses shown was when

I'd been at my worst, acting out my pain, lost in brokenness, devoid of hope and yet I was met with compassion and tender acceptance. I wasn't rebuked, harshly treated or rejected.

It was at that moment I began to see hope like a light pointing the way. A voice inside me said, *This is not who you are, come out of there and be known.* This has been my experience of God.

I'm thankful to God for people who've come across my path at such times when I needed great kindness. This depth of kindness isn't just demonstrated in response to a physical need, but when someone offers love when it seems so undeserving. Can I be the person that offers this to the broken, even when I am faced with anger, rage, animosity, jealousy or judgement?

I'm not discounting the meeting of physical needs as great kindness, but I believe the Father's kindness goes even further. We need to tap into the Father's compassion for the person in front of us and act from that place. Jesus didn't just heal the sick; He restored them fully, giving back their honour, lifting off shame and dispelling the lies spoken over their lives.

Humility

There is so much that can be said about humility. There is often a misunderstanding of what humility truly is! It's not low self-esteem or false modesty, nor is it denying the truth of who we are. Humility is fully understanding who we are, our strengths and weaknesses and our identity as sons and co-heirs. It's understanding that we have nothing and cannot attain anything without Christ.

The Lord has been teaching me that it's about a heart attitude of surrender. We do not attain it but simply receive Christ's humility. As we read the story of the life of Jesus, we can see His humility threaded through His understanding of His true identity. He never denied who He was, or held back when He should have come forward, but He allowed honour and praise to go to the Father.

He put the needs of all humanity before His own and totally surrendered to the master plan of saving the human race in choosing the Cross. Therefore, it's from the place of surrender where we bow on our faces and receive the cloak of humility from our Saviour and King.

When we're clothed in this gifted garment, we will find ourselves loving people, understanding that we don't need to boost our importance or sing our own praises but prefer others. We will allow them to receive praise and readily give all credit to God, taking nothing for ourselves. We can live and love from a place of lowly surrender, loving God first, then the Bride and then the world.

The cloak of humility is put on before all other garments, giftings and ministries. It is worn next to the skin and is most like the Christ we love. Below is a poem of my journey and my understanding of what humility is.

The Path to Humility

The path to humility

Is more of Him and less of me,

To come and bow before His throne

To make this place my only home

To surrender and listen at His feet

To hear His voice so strong and sweet

To empty myself of 'me' and 'mine'

And to be filled with His love Divine

To embrace in Him my true identity

And to clothe myself in His humility.

The path is not to beat up my heart

Nor to crucify again my darker parts

But sweet surrender and relinquished control

And give to Him my heart and soul

To say, "Yes and amen" to His voice

And in my lowliness rejoice.

And so, I choose this path to Him

To prostrate myself before the King.

Honesty

When we think of honesty, we think of being truthful: owning up to our misdemeanours, not lying to cover our tracks or gain something dishonestly. I want to go further and talk about honesty in the context of loving God, ourselves and each other. Of course we shouldn't be deceitful with one another, but dishonesty is also the lies we believe or the truths we hide from. For example, how many of us say "Yes" when we mean "No", because we're not wanting to hurt someone's feelings or let them down, all in the name of love?

Growing up, I learned to conform to my parent's wishes and demands. I loved them and desired their love and acceptance, but I conformed out of fear of being rejected, punished or unloved. I believed that love was conditional and dependent on my goodness. As a teenager, I could no longer bear to be enslaved in this way and so I rebelled.

When I became a Christian, I wanted to please God and be accepted into the church. I believed that to be 'good' was to conform. I had believed a lie! Why is conformity wrong? Surely we need to be true to God's Word and be obedient to our parents, leaders and so on? Conformity is born from fear and a need to fit in, be acceptable and loved; it is a worldly value.

Romans 12:2 (AMP) says, *"And do not be conformed to this world [any longer with its superficial values and customs], but be transformed and progressively changed [as you mature spiritually] by the renewing of your mind [focusing on godly values and ethical attitudes]"*. We all understand about living uprightly and adopting Godly attitudes, but a laid down lover drills deeper, to the core, rooting out everything that doesn't fall in line with God's truth.

God desires surrender, not conformity. We are to make decisions out of submission, from a place of love and honour for God and His people. We do this by transforming our minds by His Word and voice, as we sit at His feet and hear what He has to say about Himself, His Bride and the world.

There are many ways we can lie about our own hearts. We can ignore certain niggles that sit beneath the surface. For example, we know that particular people can irritate us, but in the name of love and 'Christian fellowship' we try to ignore or deny it! This is an opportunity to come before God and ask Him to search our hearts and reveal the log in our eyes. It could simply be that they're touching on a raw nerve that needs tending to.

We can look at the offence head-on and ask God to help us explore the root. Often it's nothing to do with the person, but the offence has touched on a much deeper pain. From that place, we can receive healing, forgiveness and restoration. Other times, it's something about the person that doesn't sit right within us and the Holy Spirit can teach us to pray in love for them. When we next speak to that person, it will then be from a place of pure love!

There may be many lies we believe but we only need to repent and receive the truth. When we learn the truth, we can see and hear what He sees and so love from the right perspective. Many of us walk around wounded and cannot give and receive love in those areas of pain. Much of our pain stems from the lies we've believed and when we fully embrace the truth and let it permeate our souls, we can truly burn with love in those areas.

Honour

We honour when we place worth or value on someone, looking for the good and the Godliness. It starts by placing value on the attributes of God's character and then finding these attributes in each other. In valuing these things, we call it out and attribute reverence to it. For example, my husband is one of the kindest people I know and offers help and compassion to others at the expense of himself. It's something I really value in him.

A few years ago, I was struggling with unforgiveness towards someone. I wanted to forgive but the sting of the hurt hindered me. The Holy Spirit said, "Instead of thinking about this hurt, why don't you look at what they have done well, how they have loved you and think about that instead?". I began thinking about those good things and I spoke them out.

My mind shifted and I began to value the relationship. I was able to put away the slight and love the Godliness in that person. It's not always easy, it takes discipline, choice and the power of the Spirit. I most often choose honour and when I don't, the Holy Spirit reminds me. The more I choose to honour, the brighter the flame will burn. I would encourage you to adopt the Kingdom approach, which is to recognise the value of the person standing in front of you.

A person doesn't earn honour by their efforts, we are to hear and see what the Father sees in that person. We freely give honour to the honourable parts in each other. When we struggle, the Holy Spirit will reveal the Godly attributes in that person. We then get to speak that over them. The good news is, the more time we spend in the Presence of the King, gazing into His beautiful countenance, the more we allow His whispers in our hearts, the easier it will be to love in this way.

Graciousness

A gracious person lets others go first, offers help and prefers other's needs to their own. They are someone who'll overlook the faults of others, showing mercy when faced with immaturity or weakness. A gracious act is to show kindness and forgiveness, overlooking the failings of others, showing empathy for those who are less mature or weaker than yourself. It's showing consideration of other's feelings, ensuring that all feel included and loved.

Graciousness is to understand the difficulties of physical and mental weaknesses and to ensure we offer support to one another. One of the attributes of God that is so often spoken of in the Word, is His graciousness. When we look at this attribute, we see how God is forgiving and kind, for He knows our weakness and our inability.

One way we can act graciously is to cover another's weakness with our strength so they aren't exposed and in that way, we strengthen the Body by supporting one another. I'm not talking about ignoring disobedience or sin, but kindly and gently covering one another's weak areas as we grow up together.

We know how to do this in the natural; for example, my taller son can reach up to the high shelves for me, when I cannot reach them. However, the Holy Spirit can show us how to do this in all areas of life! Three times, Proverbs (NIV) mentions the significance of speaking graciously to one another:

"gracious words are pure in his sight" Proverbs 15.26

"gracious words promote instruction" Proverbs 16.21

"Gracious words are a honeycomb, sweet to the soul and healing to the bones" Proverbs 16:24

How much easier is it for us to receive instruction and correction when the words spoken are gracious and laced with kindness? I love that gracious words are likened to the sweetness of honeycomb and how our hearts are rested and comforted by gracious words. When we're spoken to in a courteous, considerate and kindly manner, we feel loved and valued and our spirits lift.

As we build one another up by our gracious attitude, actions and words, we create a safe place to grow and learn together as the family of God. We need to leave space to make mistakes and learn from them as we reach full maturity, not seeing failure as weakness but as an opportunity for God to teach and empower us individually and collectively.

Generosity of Spirit

For most of us, when we think of generosity we think of it in financial terms but it is so much more. Generosity is being moved with compassion and mercy, being intentional in acts of love and building up those around us. It is an openness and willingness to share what we have and who we are with others freely, without hope or expectation of anything in return, even gratitude and praise.

Being generous is loving to see others achieve and succeed, to see them fly and overcome difficulties in their lives. It is also being forgiving and gentle, offering help, praising others and giving them the credit. We need the Holy Spirit to transform our hearts so that we can offer acts of kindness, notice opportunities to be generous, motivated to give not just money, but of ourselves.

We can listen to those who need to be heard, pray for those who need prayer, show grace and forgiveness to all, especially those we find a little harder to love. Not all destitute people walk around in rags, there are many who are emotionally or spiritually poor: broken, weak, flawed, hiding behind a well-put-together facade.

Giving money is one way to show generosity to others, especially those in financial need, but it's also God's desire that we bless each other with our time, energy, gifts and hearts, for that is truly of worth. Sometimes this will be sacrificial as God will put us in the way of true need. Sacrifice isn't from a place of striving.

As we allow our hearts to be tuned into the Holy Spirit, we'll be willing to offer what's needed to the person in front of us. We are called to love people in their brokenness and weakness, just as our gracious, benevolent, Heavenly Father. When we spend time in His Presence, being loved by Him, it's easier for us to be generous of spirit for we overflow with Him.

When we've spent time in His heart, we begin to understand how He feels, not just about us but about all mankind. As we are tuned into the heart of God, we're able to look with His eyes at what is needed and follow His lead in obedience. Romans 8:22 (TPT) says, *"Truly, deep within my true identity, I love to do what pleases God"*.

Paul states in this verse, that even when we desire to live this way, we're hindered by ourselves. Yet God has provided the way. Jesus paid the price so that the Law is fulfilled and we receive grace to walk in obedience. It's not human effort that enables us to love as

God does but the empowering of the Holy Spirit. We say, "Yes, Lord", from our true identity and He gives us everything we need. He isn't looking for our efforts but our "Yes".

---

[6] Nouwen, H. (2009). *The Way of the Heart: The Spirituality of the Desert Fathers and Mothers*. HarperOne: New York.

Living for the Audience of One

"Love the Lord your God with every passion of your heart, with all the energy of your being, and with every thought that is within you."
Matthew 22:37 (TPT)

The first thing I noticed as I read this verse, was that this is how God loves us. It's not that God is an egomaniac or has a great need to be loved, no! He is love and lives in perfect union as the Trinity. The truth is that He's a Father crying out to His creation, "I want a love-relationship with you! I created you to love and be loved!".

In Matthew 22:37-40, Jesus summed up all the laws and religious rules that were enslaving people, into two commandments. We are to love God the way He loves us. As I spoke to Jesus about loving Him in this way, He directed me to read Song of Songs 8:

"Fasten me upon your heart as a seal of fire forevermore. This living, consuming flame will seal you as my prisoner of love. My passion is stronger than the chains of death and the grave, all consuming as the very flashes of fire from the burning heart of God. Place this fierce, unrelenting fire over your entire being.

Rivers of pain and persecution will never extinguish this flame. Endless floods will be unable to quench this raging fire that burns within you. Everything will be consumed. It will stop at nothing as you yield everything to this furious fire until it won't even seem to you like a sacrifice anymore." Song of Songs 8:6-7 (TPT)

We can fulfil this commandment by allowing His love to burn within us like a raging fire, fuelled by passion and desire. As we allow His passion to consume us, we surrender in bliss and bring Him pleasure. This is our greatest calling and destiny, to bring bliss to the Great Almighty. We can move the heart and gaze of God by responding in passion to His passion for us.

Jesus died to make it possible for us to come with confidence before the Father and delight Him with who we are! We can live this life pleasing Him, for His eyes only and not in the fear of man, selfish ambition or religion. Can you hear the Father calling to you, "Come and let us reason together"? It is not duty, religion, works, piety, or any of our own efforts that please God, rather, it's surrendering to His love for us. When I read this passage in Song of Songs, I think it's more potent and beautiful than even Shakespeare could have written. It compels me to find His love and to seek Him.

Although we do love God with our emotions, this isn't about merely an emotional love but a life laid down to love and worship only Him, to live for His pleasure and no other. That is what sent Christ to the Cross. It is why many have died a martyr's death, why missionaries have endured hardships and why men and women have faced impossible odds; they understood this love and deemed it worth living and even dying for. Are we ready to join our brothers and sisters in the company of laid down lovers?

I want to look at what it means to be a "prisoner of love". Is the King asking us to be His prisoner? Is He trying to enslave us? No, I think not. For myself, I believe I'm His prisoner because my motivation, heart's desire and longing is my love for Him and His love for me. That's the place I've come to in my life and what I live for.

When I first met Jesus, He became my Saviour and we journeyed together as He led me to the Father. During this time, He became my Friend and I learnt to trust Him as I released the things in my life that weren't His best for me. I allowed Him to rule in my life as King.

Twenty years ago, I read 'The Jesus I Never Knew'[7] by Philip Yancey, who wrote about Jesus as a Jewish man. The Holy Spirit began to reveal Jesus' humanity and Jewish heritage in a way I'd never understood before. It made me realise the truth that Jesus was not here for me and my needs but for a love-union!

Yes, He came to Earth to win me back and take my place, earning my salvation. He totally loves, rescues and redeems me but ultimately, I am here for Him. I was created for His good pleasure, to love the Father and adore the Son. I began to understand His heart and love for me and how I affected Him.

I then saw the film 'The Passion of The Christ'[8] which went to great lengths to show the suffering of Jesus for us. This greatly affected me. It broke me and showed in detail what He went through for me and my heart. I spent weeks on my knees in thankfulness, adoration and love, and that was when I fell in love with Jesus as my Kinsman Redeemer and Lover.

I didn't understand fully then that He was my Bridegroom but I was so aware of His passionate love for me and I just wanted to love Him with all of me in return. I fell in love with Him more than I ever had before and that is what imprisons me.

The Bridegroom-King makes it simple for us. In Song of Songs 8:5 (TPT), He says, *"Who is this one? Look at her now! She arises out of her desert, clinging to her beloved"*. This is us, His Redeemed Bride. She has left the barren places of her soul and all that brought her death, and she clings to the Lord. This is us as individuals and as the collective Bride of Christ.

He continues, *"I awakened your innermost being... you longed for more of me"*. He goes to great lengths to woo and call us out of the grave, gently winning us over with constant forgiveness and unconditional love. He continually rescues us and walks through our pain and mistakes. He continually exposes the lies told to us by a religious spirit, fear, life's circumstances or trauma. If only we would listen to His voice and come away with Him as He desires!

I'm aware that for the human race throughout the centuries, this has not been the love understood by them. How can we offer this love to God, or to ourselves and each other when we don't understand it? Since the Fall of man, we've been a species confused about who God is and what His love looks like. Unconditional, intense, passionate love has been too big for our little souls to understand and receive.

For many, shame shouts that they're unworthy of love, so they try to earn it. It isn't God who doesn't love us but we who've struggled to receive or give the gift of unconditional love. We can easily seek to please people, driven by our need to belong, be accepted and found lovable. Yet all this is futile and we have wounded each other along the way in our broken state!

The beautiful truth is that God made it possible for us to sit on His knee in total, mutual adoration, where all striving is left outside the door like muddy boots. Paul prayed that the Holy Spirit would give us the insight and understanding to grasp *"the great magnitude of the astonishing love of Christ in all its dimensions. How deeply intimate and far-reaching is his love! How enduring and inclusive it is! Endless love beyond measurement that transcends our understanding"* (Ephesians 3:18-19 TPT).

We need help in understanding that we are wholly loved and adored despite our mess. Jesus always picks up after us and in return we get to surrender, to love and be loved. What are we waiting for? Now is the time to wake up and realise how wonderfully and passionately loved we are and to fall on our faces in response, casting our crowns, our best triumphs and our greatest victories before the King of Kings!

This has been my journey over the last thirty years, to leave my grave clothes and to stand in the marvellous light of His love and grace. These grave clothes aren't just the painful areas of my heart, but the areas of striving or living from a lie. I used to live in stress and striving because I didn't understand I could live loved and from a place of rest. There are no ought-to's or should's, just the desire to live in love with the Bridegroom-King who longs for my heart.

Song of Songs 8:8-10 (TPT) says that when the Shulamite left her barren places behind, she replied, *"I have grown and become a bride, and my love for him has made me a tower of passion and contentment for my beloved... This is how he sees me—I am the one who brings him bliss, finding favor in his eyes"*. This is for every human on the planet, whoever you are; no one is exempt.

If God says all are welcome, who are we to discount ourselves? Once we understand and accept this and begin the journey of living from this place of love, then we'll desire to live for the audience of One. Selfish ambition and fear will be drowned out by the duet of the Bride and Groom.

As we leave behind works of man, human effort, living for affirmation and praise from one another, we'll begin to soar in our attempts to make Father God smile. We can look for His gaze over our lives. We admit our mistakes and run free from condemnation as we grow in our belief that we are so dearly loved, and that it's our heart's motivation the Father sees.

He isn't looking for success as we understand it, He's looking for our growth as we journey with Him through the hills and valleys. He watches our heart's response in our greatest triumphs and deepest failures. It's not about success but the relationship that we pursue with Him.

Luke 7 shows Jesus going to the house of Simon, the Pharisee. While He is sitting at the table, a woman who's a known prostitute comes into the house and takes a beautiful, alabaster jar filled with expensive perfume. She comes to Jesus and weeps, wetting His feet with her tears which she wipes with her hair.

She kisses His feet over and over in gratitude and love. Then she opens the flask and anoints Him with her perfume, filling the room with the expensive and extravagant fragrance as an act of worship. In his misunderstanding, the religious leader thinks, *"If this man were a prophet, he would know who is touching him and what kind of woman she is—that she is a sinner"* (Luke 7:39 NIV).

Jesus explains that the woman's motivation is her value for Christ's forgiveness and love. She does what Simon does not do; she honours Jesus, pouring out her tears and worship, showing Him the proper honour and worth. Once she has finished weeping, she's able to anoint Him with her costly perfume.

The religious spirit condemned this extravagant display of vulnerability and worship. Let us never succumb to religion, tradition, fear, pride, or anything that would stop us from worshipping Jesus in this way! Let your love for Him be abandoned and outrageous, costly and extravagant. Let's fill the room with the fragrance of unbridled love for Him, with tears of gratitude for our weaknesses forgiven and hearts restored.

What struck me when I read this passage, was that she did this act in front of the religious leaders. We often go away to the secret place and worship Jesus. Our unbridled passion for Him does start there, but it's then from the overflow of this place of intimacy that we become so abandoned to Him that we have no regard for where we are or who is looking on.

This woman chose to love and worship because she had the opportunity. Let's be a people who seize the opportunity to pour out extravagant love on Jesus, regardless of where we are, who is spectating, or the voices that may speak to the contrary. Let's posture ourselves in the same way as the woman with the alabaster jar.

---

[7] Yancey, P. (1995). *The Jesus I Never Knew.* Grand Rapids: Zondervan.

[8] *The Passion of the Christ.* (2004). Directed by Mel Gibson. USA: Icon Productions.

Solitude with Him

I've always been described as an extrovert and had considered that about myself as well, however, over the last few years I've come to understand that I'm more introverted than I realised. In the past, some of my desire to be with people was actually a need for belonging, acceptance and community. At times, being in company helped shut out the noise inside and take my eyes off my own turmoil.

As I've matured and learnt to draw from Him, this has become less of a need. Because I believed I was an extrovert, I would push myself to keep going, engaging, interacting and connecting with others. Of course, this is part of me and God has gifted me in that area but even though I love my community, things had to change. God took me on a journey into rest and stillness in Him. I was taught to connect first with Him in the stillness and then I'd have the capacity to give, give, give.

I realised how stressed I'd been and that by solitude, quiet walks and 'me time', I found myself again. I found the peace and rest I needed. I found that I was content on my own. The crowd had been my hiding place, not from God but from my old self. Now I could have constant companionship, eternal peace and rest in His gentle Presence.

I find now having walked this way, that I run for solitude with Him after a time of being in company. I've come to understand that I no longer *need* community but that I *desire* community. I've let go of playing to the crowd and now pursue the stillness. I can choose peace in the midst of busyness and stressful situations. I can quiet my internal world when there is noise all around me.

I desire that my true personality would shine with Jesus and all false self would die. The Holy Spirit sends a little flare up when I slip back into old habits; I'm a chatty person but as I've matured I can also be quiet and listen. Personally, I believe I give the best of myself to others when it comes from the overflow of intimate companionship with Him.

I share this testimony with you to illustrate that regardless of whether you are a noisy, busy person, or maybe quieter and more reflective, we all need to come to the place of solitude with Him to enjoy intimate fellowship. We all need to quiet our inner self, making ourselves available for Him to come and sit awhile with us.

I wrote this chapter during the first week of lockdown in the UK, in the time of the COVID-19 virus. What was seen as isolation was also an opportunity. God had been speaking to many of us ahead of this season about carving out time for solitude with Him. This has been a journey for all of us, forced to release busyness and false idols in our lives to focus on what's truly of worth. It was a simpler life for a season.

God had been gently prodding me into a place of rest and solitude with Him for almost a year, and then came the time to take it seriously. Before the lockdown, I visited a beautiful garden in Somerset which is one of my favourite places to go to relax, unwind and enjoy the beauty of nature. There were signs all around the park saying *pause, reflect, listen.*

God was clearly speaking into the season that was about to come, to step away from fear and panic, to let go of it all and build from the beginning. We needed to look at what's really valuable to us as individuals, communities, nations and more importantly, as people of God. I could busy myself with projects and plans left aside due to time restrictions, or I could become lazy and watch Netflix. He called me to a greater purpose, not busyness or laziness, but stillness.

In the stillness, we can posture our hearts to become quiet and reflective, available to listen to the whispers and promptings of God. We can really sit and think, meditating on what's being said inside our hearts. We can hold up to the light what we believe about ourselves, Him and the world.

It's important to not just read the Word but meditate on it and map it onto our lives, motives, plans, character and beliefs so that we become quiet, teachable, reflective and receptive, our hearts searching for His. We get to create a culture where we lead the way back to "Who am I being?" not "What am I doing?".

The practise of silence: where there is no worship or soaking music, no podcast playing, just the sweet silence. I'm not saying any of those things are wrong. They have merit and a place for us in today's culture but it can become very easy to surround ourselves with noise and drown out the silence. Why are so many of us afraid of solitude?

It's when we sit still that we can hear life going on all around us; the sounds of nature and people moving throughout their day. All of that becomes white noise when we're busy with life, so how much more with the voice of God? Let's not drown out the whispers of God with inferior noise.

In the silence, our own voice can be heard. Sometimes it's not something we want to hear, however, it's a chance to listen to ourselves. Don't mistake this with self-pity but use sober judgement to listen to your own body and heart, practising self-care. It's in this place we make space for God to speak. We can then leave the shores of 'me, myself and I' and journey with Him to His heart.

In the silence, we quiet down the voices that have vied for our attention and we listen. We hush the thoughts that want to invade. I liken this practice to the times I had to quiet down my children when they were small so that my husband could speak. All of them felt they had something important to say but there are times when it's more important to listen to the voice of a father.

Let's hear what our Father has to say over the many other voices, for He is the only one who can be fully trusted to always speak the truth in love. When we allow silence, we hear that still, small voice that wants us to come away with Him. The place He wants to take us is solitude with Him.

In Mark 6:30-32 (TPT), the Disciples had been busy following Jesus in obedience but they were tired and hungry with no respite; *"So Jesus said to his disciples, 'Come, let's take a break and find a secluded place where you can rest a while.' They slipped away and left by sailboat for a deserted spot"*. What a beautiful picture. We can imagine ourselves floating away on a sailboat with Jesus to a secluded place to rest awhile with Him.

"Solitude is the furnace of transformation. Without solitude we remain victims of our society and continue to be entangled in the illusions of the false self... Solitude is the place of the great struggle and the great encounter - the struggle against the compulsions of the false self, and the encounter with the loving God who offers himself as the substance of the new self." - Henri J.M. Nouwen [9]

The great struggle is where self has to die: lies are exposed, all false-self behaviours are unmasked, old mindsets are revealed and our character laid bare. Is it any wonder we run from solitude with God? To stand before Him, naked in this way, means death to our old man. The truth is, He's known all along the things that remained hidden, it is we who get a shock!

He comes in love to cut off everything that hinders us. He challenges everything in us that stands against Him or in place of Him; our false idols topple along with our false self. It's then He's able to reign supreme within us. When we hear and accept the hard truths about ourselves, it leads to our betterment and makes room for more of Him. This is the salvation won for us.

Our great encounter with the Father. He is all love, all compassion and all-knowing. He is ever-faithful and trustworthy and loves us best. Surely we want every part of us to experience Father God in this way? He adopts and embraces us and calls us close. There we receive His nurture, comfort, rest and peace.

He invites us to come and know Him better, to understand we are fully known and loved. Let me say this again, *we are invited to know the Almighty God in intimacy as Father and child!* This replaces and supersedes any earthly relationship with a father, leader or teacher, especially if they didn't represent the Father well. We can now gaze upon the true Father.

Our great encounter with Jesus. King Yeshua! He is our beautiful Saviour, our Lord and Friend. He is our Brother, our true Lover and Bridegroom. He will show us His passionate pursuit and embrace, His constant wooing and longing for our hearts, and how His life was given in exchange for ours. He'll reveal to us His jealous and zealous refusal to share us with another. He is our true Champion and Deliverer.

Our great encounter with the Holy Spirit. He is our beautiful Counsellor, Friend, Guide, Teacher and Mother. He is the best of friends, the kindest parent and teacher. He is our only Life-coach and will always lead us and direct our steps. He lives in our bones and dwells within our flesh, if we only ask Him. He is always present, always speaking gently to us, showing us the way to the Father and Jesus.

He reminds us who we are and who we are not, and constantly recounts the truth about the Trinity. We can receive from Him the revelation light to see and hear, being led back to the still waters, the place of rest.

Our great encounter with the Trinity. We can exist in the midst of the Father, Son and Holy Spirit. When we encounter this experience, the only thing we can see and hear is God in community and unity, family in its truest form. Here we are truly safe, completely loved and fully restored. We lack nothing here, for there is a feasting table set before us where we share the delights laid out with Almighty God. Our needs are met and all suffering and lack are forgotten. Let's hunger and thirst for this encounter and to understand God in this way.

For those who have been going deeper, the practice of solitude is a call to go deeper still, to dig out the treasures and make a pathway for others to follow. We can share from our overflow and provoke a desire in others to go seek, that those who hunger would be fed and then hunger for more!

If we practice solitude now, we'll develop a lifestyle that will serve us in the busy seasons. We'll have established the pattern of taking a breath and pausing to reflect on Him, our present season, our life goals and decisions. We can listen to His perspective, to His choices for us and the life He has for us.

As we practice solitude, we will reflect Him. If you think of how a prism refracts light to reveal the colours of the rainbow, we too can display the colours of His nature and so He will be seen through us.

In the Silence

I quieten my heart to hear the King

No tumble of words or songs to sing

I sit in the silence, my heart open wide

And I wait for the still, small voice inside.

The whisper, the breath, the Presence; it's Him!

The arrival of God, my Father, my King.

No books are read, no sermon spoken,

Just my heart laid bare and my soul awoken.

I listen for the whisper, the voice, the song

I hear the heartbeat of the Father and the breath of the Son.

In the Silence you move…

And truth is revealed and my life is revived.

My heart is healed and my soul comes alive

As I surrender and listen for the whisper within.

No noise or words, just the Presence of Him.

---

[9] Nouwen, H. (2009). *The Way of the Heart: The Spirituality of the Desert Fathers and Mothers.* HarperOne: New York.

So this is Life

As we begin to understand Creator God, it should greatly affect the way we live our lives and how we respond to others. What reaction and action do we take when faced with life's hurdles? This is not a 'how-to' chapter, as the Holy Spirit is the best Advisor for each one of us; I do, however, want to look at what it means to live this way every day.

I got saved in the 1980s during the Charismatic Movement. It was a time of beginning to understand the Holy Spirit and His empowering for the Body of Christ. It was a thrilling time to be part of God's people. I was spiritually starving and went to as many meetings that were available. Healing meetings, worship meetings, prayer meetings, bible studies; most of my evenings and weekends were filled with searching for God and His people.

When other teenagers were going off to parties and clubbing holidays, I was going to Spring Harvest and worship concerts. I wanted to be in the centre of it all but I was a baby in the Kingdom and I lived two disjointed lives. One I lived for Him and His people, and the other was a dark side of bad choices, unresolved pain and love for the world.

It was this journey and my relationship with God that has been teaching me how to live everyday life. Every moment we choose Him, we experience His love and our hearts are won over piece by piece. This is our decision and we are never forced to follow. It's God who knocks continually on the doors of our hearts. For most of us, it's not hard-heartedness that keeps us away but distraction, busyness and even a lack of discipline.

What's helped me live every day with Him at the centre, is learning what it means to live abiding in the Vine and then taking those experiences, encounters and revelations with me everywhere I go. What does it mean to live in the Vine? It is to live grafted into Jesus Christ.

In John 15, Jesus urges His disciples to remain in Him. He explains that His fruit is demonstrated in our lives when we abide in Him, which means to consistently live in and with Him. Jesus expects and challenges us to abide in Him and for His words to abide in us. So what does this look like? To abide is to stay stable or fixed, to make our home in Him, live our lives in Him and to remain. When we do this, we allow the Vine to become our life-source, allowing Him to feed and sustain us.

Abiding means we spend our time thinking about and talking to Jesus, involving Him in our everyday decisions. It's not just living with Him but allowing Him to live within *us* so that we're connected to His voice wherever we are. Even when we feel low, distracted, depressed, angry or hurt, we don't need to turn away from Him but invite Him into those spaces and talk through what we're facing and feeling.

He never condemns us, nor sends us away when we don't feel peace, joy, love, hope and faith. It's at these times He embraces us and draws us in, if only we would let Him. Just think how different it would be if you invited Him into your moments of disappointment, rejection, betrayal or failure.

When we're grafted into the Vine, not only are we connected into Him but we're also connected into each other. It would be a poor vine if it only had one branch, surviving alone! We are to be grafted in as the Church, the Body, the Bride, the Ekklesia. We dwell alongside each other, drawing from the same Source. As we abide together, we can spur one another on to grow, sharing revelation and feasting together. We can be grafted into the Vine, finding His Presence and receiving His gift of relationship.

Jesus also said His words need to remain in us. This means that when we read the Word of God, when we hear prophetic words spoken over our lives or receive revelation from Him, we are to take hold of and think about those things, meditating on them. We can use our reason, understanding and imagination, coming to Him to comprehend on a deeper level. We can study with Him as our Tutor.

We can sit at His feet as He speaks truth and wisdom into our hearts and minds. We are to map His words over our life to see how it fits into His ways and plans. We can ask questions of the Father and the Holy Spirit. We can also ask ourselves questions like, *How does this word apply to me today? How does it apply to my life, my family, my community, my workplace?*

I find it invaluable to keep a journal in which I write Bible verses God has shown me and prophetic words I've received, with my thoughts and responses. I also write a dialogue between myself and God. I allow my imagination to be used by God to speak to me about what I'm reading or listening to, and I'll then write out what I've experienced. This means I have a written record of what God has said and is saying to me personally.

I also find it useful to go back months or even years before to see the journey I've been on. There are times when I've seen God was literally saying the same thing over and over again until the penny dropped. It's not just about having a record, which is of course useful, but writing it out has helped me process what I'm receiving in those moments. You might like to type or even record your voice; whichever way we journal, we can remind ourselves of what He's said and can also ask the Holy Spirit to show us if there's anything we've forgotten.

I believe, if we've truly taken in what He's spoken to us, then these words will echo through our minds like someone calling through the halls of a great house. Our spirits and souls are nourished by His words. We can be fed over and over again. The Bible is life-giving and points us to the Father, His Son and the beautiful call to intimacy; it gives us hope, wisdom and answers.

When we surrender and bow the knee to Him, it's because we've heard the heartfelt cry for relationship. If we choose this way of life, we can live inside of God: the Almighty, all-powerful, God of the Universe! This is the best invitation we will ever get. If we spent our days living in a barrel of wine, we would always smell like the wine, being saturated in it wherever we went. In the same way, let's be soaked and immersed in Jesus.

If we are grafted into Him, we'll always be alive and bearing fruit. This fruit will be His fruit and is to be given away to everyone else. We will produce Jesus-fruit, fruit that is so sweet and sustaining, fruit that blesses and tastes like love, compassion, hope and joy.

To Abide

A lifestyle of abiding is to draw from Your Goodness,

To dwell in Your Presence, drinking from Your love

To think Your thoughts as I encounter life

To feel with Your heart when I encounter people

To live from You, for You, with You and in You.

A conversation of friendship as I learn to be kind

To listen to Your heart and see with your eyes

To engage and encounter, to laugh, cry and embrace

To speak out Your words and to act with Your grace

To go from You, for You, with You and in You.

As I step out of my door, the secret place still within,

My sanctuary of peace on the move.

I will see Your wonder in the everyday

The likeness of Jesus in those I meet

To love from You, for You, with You and in You.

What does it look like to live in a deeper level of abiding in Him? On one occasion, I asked the Father what it would be like to be inside His heart. As I did so, I saw myself being embraced by Him and then pulled in deeper so that I was inside the very heart of God. There was such safety and peace there. I was so very well hidden but I also understood it was a dangerous place to dwell if I wanted to hold onto my old self.

The Holy Spirit said, "You are here by invitation but if you want to remain here you need to let go of all offence; to remain here is to put aside all pain, wounding, brokenness, and all unhealed and unresolved areas of your heart". In short, everything had to come into alignment with God's heart. I could not afford to hold onto anything that didn't look or sound like Him.

I'm not saying we need to be perfect to dwell within the heart of God, no, we are made perfect in Him as we allow His heart to realign us with the truth. It's here we learn the Heavenly language of love that sounds very different to our old nature. Abiding inside the heart of the Father empowers us to be loved with perfect love and to accept that we are fully loved. When we receive His love, we are then able to love Him in return. We can also then love ourselves and others with His love.

We need to understand that this invitation is for the whole world, that everyone is invited to live within the very walls of God. This is the destiny God has for each of us. Once I'd had this conversation with the Holy Spirit, it became increasingly difficult to carry offence or continue to walk outside of love. If I did, it would mean stepping outside the heart of God.

The good news is, if we remain and abide inside the heart of God, His heartbeat and love become ours. Is this not a place where we would all want to live? By abiding here, we begin to understand what true love is and live from that place. We cannot love outside of God and so the closer we get to His heart, the easier it is to live not only loved but to live as a lover. There is grace for this! We can pursue God and dwell inside His heart. From that place, He teaches us how to love well.

Not only can we abide in the heart of God but we can abide in the mind of Christ. This means every thought, mindset and belief is interviewed by the truth. If it doesn't sound like Christ, it needs to leave! We guard our minds by submitting to His truth. We hold up every thought pattern, conversation and belief, and command it to come into alignment with Him.

It's this simple: every chance we get, we can ask Christ His perspective and listen for His truth and wisdom. The Holy Spirit will always expose deception and any false information. We have all spent time being bombarded by the Liar, however, we choose truth when we choose Jesus. As we remain here, we can come humbly to the God of all truth and wisdom and receive the freedom that He brings.

The fiercest battles are won and lost in the mind, but when our Saviour's voice is heard it deafens any lie. This is so simple that even little children excel at it: ask God, believe He speaks the truth and then live in it, denying anything that does not match up. Let's abide in Christ, living and believing in His truth and love.

When we abide in God, we can leave the smallness of our lives behind and pursue the bigness of His Kingdom. We'll no longer be satisfied with crumbs but will hunger for God's feast. In the natural, when we're entering adulthood, we begin to long for a bigger, more fulfilling life where we can leave home and explore the world. So it is when we're no longer children in the Kingdom but mature sons, we long for the adventure of His Kingdom coming in our lives and this world.

How do we transition from the secret place, those precious, quiet moments of revelation and freedom and those special times of intimacy and worship? How does that relate to our everyday lives? We understand how precious it is to turn off our phones, close the door and spend time with the Father, Son and the Holy Spirit. We understand how important those times are when we dig into the Word and come before Him, longing for His Presence within us. Outside of this, we need to have continual engagement with Him, not just in those special encounters but in the moment-by-moment walking of our lives.

I love the encounters that so change us on the inside that we know we'll never be the same again, when we are kissed awake by the Son or swept up by the Father. I call this 'the secret place on the move' because we need to learn to move and live in that moment with Him.

We need His voice reverberating inside of us, the internal conversation that guides, corrects, directs and speaks wisdom. When we live like this, we begin to see with the eyes of His love because we are so loved, so ravished on the inside that we no longer operate from fear or selfishness. Wherever we are and whoever we meet, we'll look into the eyes of love as we see the imager-bearer of God in everyone we come across.

Because we know and are fully known, we walk and rest in that love. We can take with us the secret garden of the secret place. We can have encounters as we go about our day wherever we are. This isn't just for the few. This invitation is for everyone, for all mankind!

We are given a choice to become a laid down lover. This isn't just in the moments that we find available but all of the time. When we're waiting for the bus, or for an appointment, or when we can only see another grey day, we can turn inward to the Holy Spirit and enter into the internal discussion. We can ask Him His thoughts and plans for our lives.

Especially after a busy weekend, Monday mornings used to sometimes feel like a drag, whether it was traipsing to work, taking my kids to school, or facing the household chores. On my way to work, I used to jump off the bus a few stops early so I could walk and talk about the day ahead with the Holy Spirit. Instead of dreading the day or just going through the motions, I used to ask for His perspective and embrace the day with all its favour, blessings, goodness, love and secrets to be shared.

I'd also ask for the life lessons and the encounters with people that God had planned out for me before I was born. This meant I arrived at the office ready for the day with a big smile on my face, bringing in an atmosphere of His Presence.

Sometimes, during a difficult or stressful day, I would need to be reminded that each day was a blessing and even in the tough moments there was peace, grace, blessing and favour. It also meant I was able to see everyone and everything around me from the Father's perspective. From that place, I was able to be a conduit for God's love, peace, joy and wisdom.

I've taken this lesson with me and even though I now work from home, I still have the choice to look up, seek His face and Kingdom, and not just focus on my wants and needs. By doing this, I bless His heart as He blesses mine. When I spend time gazing upon His face, I wonder why I'm not always rushing to linger in His Presence instead of concerning myself with the smallness of my own heart and mind.

"For better is one day in your courts than a thousand elsewhere."
Psalm 84:10 (NIV)

When you're in love with someone, you think about them all the time. You can't wait to hear their voice or see their face. When I was dating my husband, we would spend hours on the phone even if we'd seen each other that day. I didn't want to hang up because I wanted more than anything to hear his voice and I couldn't wait for the next time I'd see him. That's how all God-lovers feel about God. The best thing is, we don't have to wait for His phone call!

We don't have to wait for the meetings or the conferences. We can come before Him whenever we want and have that conversation. We can't manufacture or manifest an encounter, that comes from Him, but we can make ourselves available for Him. Turning off our phones and closing the door, laying down all distractions and making ourselves available, we can open the door to the secret place and catch His eye.

We can carry not just the memory of our time with Him but a posture of availability. Wherever we are and wherever we go, He is within us and His voice resounds within our bones. If our bodies truly are a temple of the Holy Spirit, then like the days of the Old Testament when the tabernacle and Ark of the Covenant were on the move with the people of God, the new tabernacle is on the move within us.

Can you imagine what the Bride of Christ would look like if everyone understood the reality of carrying the secret place inside of us: His Presence! The interaction of His love and our love is exchanged within our flesh. This love affair is taking place 24/7. His love is provoking our love and our love is ravishing His heart, and so this relationship goes back and forth. What a day it will be when the world sees the lovesick Bride!

I love weddings, when you see a bride and groom announcing their love for one another unashamedly in public. It's an intimate and private relationship, yet on that day it's shared and celebrated. Everyone gets to partake in the joy of their love and witness the covenant they make with one another.

What a beautiful picture of our love-relationship with King Jesus, who has made a covenant with us and waits as the Bridegroom for us. He waits for our "Yes", as we come to the altar in surrender, giving all of ourselves to Him: body, soul and spirit forever and ever. For all eternity we are His and He is ours.

When we spend time in the secret place, when we live from the Father's lap, when we understand what is to die to self, to let the seven flames of love burn and to live grafted into the Vine, we will then be able to take the treasure within us everywhere we go and the overflow will spill out all around us to others. This is our destiny.

When there is a whole company of laid down lovers, then the world will notice and be taken hold of by love. God loves the world and He wants to show that love through His people.

It's time for us to be the Bride and carry His Presence within us, not that we give away those intimate moments with the Lord but that we share the fruit and the overflow of our love exchange. Such joy, such bliss, such tender love, compassion and His faithfulness. All this will be woven into everything we do and say. Of course we aren't perfect in this yet, that will come. For now, we ask the Holy Spirit to work through us, that the fruits of the secret place encounter will spill out and we will shine like stars.

Passionate Pursuit

"How deep is God's love? He gives himself to those who have made a place for Him." - Madame Guyon

"we make it our life's passion to live our lives pleasing to him" 2 Corinthians 5:9 (TPT)

Our moments are to be filled with Him, seeking Him out, moving ourselves both in mind and heart towards Him. This isn't from a place of striving but falling into a deep place of rest and love. We let go of all sorrow, darkness, failure, fear, brokenness and self, leaving behind all self-gratification, comfort, solace, self-protection and self-preservation. We lay down all accolades, trophies, awards, praise and fear of man.

In our divine nakedness, we pursue the One who makes our hearts sing. We don't pursue Him for blessing, nor healing or provision. Nor do we look for reward or favour. Our reward is His face turned towards us, His eyes shining as His lips curl into a smile. His mouth opens wide and sends out a laugh of joy because we are here, standing before Him. Then we see that we're not naked but clothed in His beauty; His righteousness and holiness adorn us as we're enveloped in His glory and delight.

We stand royal, we stand bridal, we stand as shining ones before the face of God. The same face that took every beating that was ours, the face that cried tears for us. The One who knew tiredness, betrayal, hardship, misunderstanding, insult and our shame and weakness. It is the same face that shines, full of life, hope, joy, laughter, victory, power and majesty. That is our very rich reward!

We stand before Him and receive every good gift and a crown of beauty. As we stand before Him, we then fall on our faces, laying all before Him for we have received the greatest treasure of all. We've received the dancing twinkle in His eyes of love, so much acceptance and loving approval. We can embrace God and in turn, we get to reflect Him!

"My darling bride, my private paradise, fastened to my heart... A secret spring are you that no one else can have Your inward life is now sprouting, bringing forth fruit. What a beautiful paradise unfolds within you." Song of Songs 4:12-14 (TPT)

I would encourage you to read the whole of Song of Songs 4, as the King describes His response to us, His beloved, as we surrender and worship Him. Jesus highly values our inner life with Him. It's such a sacred and precious place. It's where perfect union begins, where He leads and we follow.

The garden found in the Song of Songs is the inner relationship between us and God. The fruits are the places in our hearts that have surrendered and allowed the King in to redeem and restore. It's the Father who has planted seeds to bear fruit inside of us, so that we may reveal His nature and His likeness.

We may have allowed our fruitfulness to be overshadowed by the cares of the world or the belief that we couldn't possibly please His heart, yet He speaks of our garden with such love and delight. We no longer need to wear sackcloth and ashes for our nakedness, nor do we cover ourselves with the fig leaves of shame.

We cannot earn our place by His side. It is Christ Himself who clothes us in righteousness. It is His Spirit who toils alongside us in our paradise garden, producing the fruit spoken of in Song of Songs. It starts with finding ourselves at the Cross.

"And by the blood of his cross, everything in heaven and earth is brought back to himself—back to its original intent, restored to innocence again... his own body as the sin-payment on your behalf so that you would dwell in his presence. And now there is nothing between you and Father God, for he sees you as holy, flawless, and restored." Colossians 1:20-22 (TPT)

We are no longer sin-drenched, desperately covering the shame handed down through generations from that moment in the garden of Eden. This is a beautiful beginning to our love story, where our victory has been won for us and our identity restored. If we read on past the Crucifixion, we see the Church bursting forth in glory and the Bride emerging to meet the coming King Jesus.

This life journey is all about the pursuit of intimate connection, where our hearts are inflamed with passion as we realise how extravagantly loved we are. We must allow ourselves to believe we are relentlessly and passionately wooed and pursued. We can open our hearts to be won over by overwhelming love and in return, we relentlessly pursue the heart that is overwhelmed by us.

Jesus isn't waiting for us to be feeling a passionate desire, He is excited by any flicker of desire we have within us. Just a glance is all it takes to unravel the heart of God.

"For you reach into my heart. With one flash of your eyes I am undone by your love... You leave me breathless—I am overcome by merely a glance from your worshiping eyes, for you have stolen my heart." Song of Songs 4:9 (TPT)

In the footnotes of this chapter in The Passion Translation, Brian Simmons says, "He is saying that your loving eyes of worship have uncovered his heart and laid it bare, making him vulnerable to you. What a description of what happens to Jesus when he looks into your eyes. Your worship brings to him such an ecstasy and delight that it becomes hard to even imagine. Yet God has placed inside of you the ability to ravish the heart of your King—not someday in heaven, but now, even when you feel incomplete and weak." [10]

Ephesians 1:3-4 (TPT) says that the Father sees us wrapped up in Jesus; *"And he chose us to be his very own, joining us to himself even before he laid the foundation of the universe!"*. The triune God very much wants the intimate relationship with us we were created to have. It's not a God chasing down His created ones to fall in line in obedience and worship. He desires for us to return to our truest calling and Divine destiny, since before time began, which is that we should love and be loved.

There is a childish game called 'kiss chase', where the boys and girls take turns to chase one another and when caught, the captured one receives a kiss. In my experiences with King Jesus, I find there are times where I'm looking to please His heart, pouring out my love to Him, and other times it is He that pours out His passionate and unrelenting love for me and I am undone.

I find myself crying in gratitude and lost for words at the love that exceeds all human love. It all starts and ends with Him, for *"we love because he first loved us"* (1 John 4:19 NIV). It was Christ who won me over first and so I responded in gratitude and love, which became worship and adoration of who He is and not just what He has done.

When we enjoy intimacy with King Yeshua, we begin to see more than the Man who saved us, gave us a place in Heaven, healed our hearts and bodies, and restored our fortunes. We long for time alone with Him so that we can just be together. Sometimes there doesn't need to be words, just His Presence, and we become lovesick.

What I love about this relationship is there are no qualifications needed, no standards to be met. We cannot be holy enough, righteous enough, beautiful enough or know the right worship songs. We just need one thing: surrender!

It's as we bow down in humility and agree that He qualifies us and that all else is nothing, that we willingly open up the deepest places in our hearts and minds to Him and reach for His heart in return. We submit readily to His voice whispering to us, "Come away with me", and we sink deeply into His arms, resting our head on His chest and say, "Yes Lord".

In Song of Songs 4, the Shulamite Bride responds to the King's vulnerable admission about how she affects His heart. Let this be our heart's cry as well:

"Then may your awakening breath blow upon my life until I am fully yours. Breathe upon me with your Spirit wind. Stir up the sweet spice of your life within me. Spare nothing as you make me your fruitful garden. Hold nothing back until I release your fragrance. Come walk with me as you walked with Adam in your paradise garden. Come taste the fruits of your life in me." Song of Songs 4:16 (TPT)

Love Sick

I was heartsick before, when you called me back.

Away from the Liar and the noisy bustle of life.

You loved on me as you restored and healed all broken, jagged parts of my soul.

Your fiery, intense love burned within me, 'till the ashes revealed the beauty of You

And now my identity is restored and I am whole.

I am His and He is mine.

This love exchange is real

Not just a God-man saving sinners,

But a Lover-King wooing a Bride.

I was heartsick and now I am lovesick.

A true, bridal romance, where I have stolen His heart and He has mine

So much more perfect than we can imagine.

The ultimate love, so pure and Divine.

I want to stay in this lovesick moment, to rest here and close the door.

The world has its delights but can no way compare,

With this, this secret place.

This Space,

Where our love is exchanged.

Where I have ravished His heart too

So that He rides over the mountains, singing my name.

The intense burning in His heart for me.

A pure, jealous love that roars

For every unsurrendered part of my heart,

For He is lovesick too!

[10] Simmons, B. (2017). *The Passion Translation New Testament with Psalms, Proverbs, and Song of Songs.* Minneapolis: Broadstreet Publishing Group, Song of Songs 4:9, p.301.

Why Join the Company of Laid Down Lovers?

I have come to understand that I deeply affect the heart of God. My response to Him moves Him. The pages of the Bible sing out His love for us and as we look a little deeper, we see the heart of the Father's longing, the wooing of the King. When we choose Him and embrace the love exchange, we ravish His heart. We can serve Him faithfully but it's when we love Him in this way He's most delighted.

"you have captivated my heart with one glance of your eyes." Song of Songs 4:9 (ESV)

David made many mistakes but He loved God first and foremost. He ruled a nation and led His people in praise to God. Mary loved Jesus with such extravagance and was criticised for her behaviour because it was the opposite of religion. Can our love be as extravagant a response to the passion that He has for us? Do we desire to cast our crowns before Him? Do we desire to 'waste time' with Him?

Our Creator calls out to us, wanting connection not from a place of brokenness or need but from His desire as our Parent, our Lover and Friend. Our destiny is to spend eternity connecting with His heart. The rules of religion are gone. The striving to be worthy has ceased and the working for acceptance is done away with. It is a surrendering, a release and a falling into unconditional, overwhelming love that is the truth.

No matter who we are and how we choose to love Him, let's lay ourselves down for our King. God is waiting for your "Yes".

Who Am I?

I say, "Who am I that you would think of me?"

You reply, "I say that you are mine,

I think about you always, I think about you all the time.

You are part of me and I am part of you.

I chased you down and sought you out

And my desire for you is that your heart, with love, would shout.

Together we fit, integral to the Father's plan.

For you are to be included, to be part of the Great I AM.

I formed you in your mother's womb and laughed with delight at your start.

For I knew from the beginning I would always have your heart.

My beloved, you are my precious one. My beauty, I am your home

And I long for your attention, for your gaze to seek my own.

So when you ask, 'Who am I?'

I say, 'You're part of me, my own one, my true love.

I created you, I wooed you and taught you how to love.'"

"My heart is on fire, boiling over with passion. Bubbling up within me are these beautiful lyrics as a lovely poem to be sung for the King. Like a river bursting its banks, I'm overflowing with words, spilling out into this sacred story...Your royal robes release the scent of suffering love for your bride; the odor of aromatic incense is upon you. From the pure and shining place, lovely music that makes you glad is played for your pleasure...

And standing beside you, glistening in your pure and golden glory, is the beautiful bride-to-be! [Footnote: 'or Queen'] Now listen, daughter, pay attention, and forget about your past. Put behind you every attachment to the familiar, even those who once were close to you! For your royal Bridegroom is ravished by your beautiful brightness." Psalm 45:1,8-11 (TPT)

About the Author

Jane Gibbs is a contemporary Christian artist living in the West Country of England with her family and dog, Edgar. Saved in 1986 in London, she has spent her adult life pursuing and being pursued by the Lover of her soul. She is a woman after God's heart, a passionate lover of Jesus and a fierce lover of those who God brings to her.

Her creative soul longs to show the heart of God to others, carrying the authentic, raw and undiluted love of Jesus. She has been forged in the fire of His Presence and her scars have been kissed by the King.

After spending many years as a prophetic singer and intercessor, God called her to communicate her expression of His voice through art and poetry. Her highest calling is to live a life surrendered to the King of kings. 'The Company of Laid Down Lovers' is her first publication and describes her journey with the Lord to find her true identity and destiny.

For details on her work as an artist and poet please visit janegibbsartist.com

Printed in Great Britain
by Amazon